THE
2-HOUR
JOB SEARCH

Second Edition

THE
2-HOUR
JOB SEARCH

Second Edition

Using Technology to Get
the Right Job *FASTER*

STEVE DALTON

TEN SPEED PRESS
California | New York

All rights reserved.
Published in the United States by Ten Speed Press,
an imprint of Random House, a division of
Penguin Random House LLC, New York.
www.tenspeed.com

Ten Speed Press and the Ten Speed Press colophon
are registered trademarks of Penguin Random House LLC.

An earlier edition of this work was published in 2012
by Ten Speed Press, an imprint of Random House,
a division of Penguin Random House LLC.

Library of Congress Cataloging-in-Publication Data
  Names: Dalton, Steve, 1976- author.
  Title: The 2-hour job search: using technology to get the right job faster /
    by Steve Dalton.
  Other titles: Two hour job search
  Description: Second edition. | California : Ten Speed Press, [2020] |
    Includes bibliographical references and index.
  Identifiers: LCCN 2019052018 | ISBN 9781984857286 (trade paperback) |
    ISBN 9781984857293 (epub)
  Subjects: LCSH: Job hunting. | Job hunting--Computer network resources. |
    Career development--Computer network resources.
  Classification: LCC HF5382.7 .D35 2020 | DDC 650.14—dc23
  LC record available at https://lccn.loc.gov/2019052018.

Trade Paperback ISBN: 978-1-98485-728-6
eBook ISBN: 978-1-60774-171-8

Printed in the United States

Cover illustration copyright © Andrey Rudin/iStockphoto
Cover design by Katy Brown and Abhimanyu Sandal
Interior design by Abhimanyu Sandal

10 9 8 7 6 5 4 3 2

Second Edition

CONTENTS

In loving memory of my parents,
Thomas and Dorothy Dalton

INTRODUCTION

Technological progress has merely provided us
with more efficient means for going backwards.
—ALDOUS HUXLEY

I've heard numerous theories for why the job search is so difficult
these days: unresponsive employers, an uncertain economy, outsourc-
ing, nepotism, poor work ethic, too much reality TV. During my
decade and a half as a senior career coach and programming director
at Duke University's Fuqua School of Business, I've helped people of
all backgrounds, professions, and ages through the job search process,
and I attribute its difficulty to something else entirely—technology.

Technology has made our lives easier in so many ways, but it
has only complicated the modern-day job search. Before internet job
postings grew in popularity circa 2000, the job search was a simple
(though tedious) process:

STEP 1 (OPTIONAL). Find classified ads in newspaper.
STEP 2. Mail resume and cover letter to potential employers.
STEP 3. Wait for invitations to interview.

That doesn't sound so bad, right? Ship out resumes and cover
letters, and whoever is interested writes you back. Very straightforward. And, believe it or not, it actually worked! Of course, those
with connections to the potential employer still fared best, not having
to rely on a piece of paper to make their first impression for them;
however, cold calls by phone or mail were often all it would take to
get an interview.

1

Fast-forward a couple of decades. The internet's in full swing, websites find relevant job postings for you, and resumes can be submitted online at any hour of the day. Although it's easier than ever before to *find* jobs, why does it now seem so much harder to actually *get* one? In short, technology made applying for jobs so efficient that *hiring* became inefficient.

Technology effectively ruined the "mail and wait" job search strategy because it is now far more difficult for employers to pick out the few interesting applicants from the massive new influx of casual applicants.

Applying for jobs used to require significant time and energy to search classified ads in your local paper, type and print cover letters and resumes (or CVs, depending on your profession and part of the world—I use the terms interchangeably in this book) on nice paper, and package them up in envelopes for mailing. Not everyone had that kind of spare time and energy (or money for that matter—stationery and postage weren't cheap!), and applying to any job required at least a minimal amount of research—heading to the library to find an address to mail your CV to, for example.

With the internet, applying for a job can take less than a minute. Google a potential employer's name, click on the careers section of their website, and submit your information and resume. Done. When it's that easy, anyone can do it—and everyone does. Thus recruiters who, before internet job postings, used to get a dozen or so applications in several weeks from mostly local candidates, now get hundreds or thousands from across the country within hours.

Who has time to read hundreds of CVs? Recruiters today read resumes the way most of us read websites—ignoring a majority of what's on the page and skipping to the headlines of greatest interest—in the case of resumes, that usually means objective information like schools attended, previous employers, and job titles, if that.

That's if hiring managers actually look at CVs received online in the first place. My students commonly describe online job postings as black holes, and I agree. Because there is no way for a hiring manager to read all those applications, the only fair thing to do is not read any of them, so they may avoid online applicants entirely. (That this attitude saves a hiring manager many hours of additional work is hardly coincidental!) Employers these days rely instead on internal referrals to decide whom to interview.

Research backs this up. According to one study, for every one position the New York Federal Reserve filled with an online job posting applicant, they filled twelve through internal referrals.[1]

Put another way, every time you apply for a job online, not only are you hoping to be one of the handful of applicants employers choose to speak to out of the hundreds who apply, you're also hoping that it's the one in thirteen that will be filled by an online applicant rather than an internal referral. The odds are nearly insurmountable. Pouring more hours into online applications is the equivalent of trying to pay your rent by buying even more lottery tickets. It may work once in a blue moon, but that doesn't make it a good approach.

Getting internal referrals is simply the only predictable way to get interviews; getting them *efficiently* is the core challenge of the modern job search.

This book is effectively a "speedrun" approach for completing that core challenge. Speedrunning is a video-gaming hobby where players record themselves trying to finish video games in world-record times by combining world-class reflexes and concentration with a deep knowledge of quirks and vulnerabilities in each video game's programming. Interestingly, it is a communal process rather than a competitive one; once one player identifies a new shortcut, every other player can now adopt that shortcut to improve their own times, further raising the bar. Similarly, this revised edition of *The 2-Hour Job Search* (2HJS for short) is itself informed by the thousands of readers, users, and practitioners who read the original edition and contributed their own shortcuts to the process. In that sense, we are all now standing on the shoulders of giants, and by considering the steps outlined in this book, you are joining a community that is eager to share their own best practices for this process with you.

Before we proceed further, a quick disclaimer: **The titular two hours refers to the amount of time it takes to lay the**

groundwork for your process, not the totality of your job search. That said, once your foundation is in place, the remaining steps in your search become seamless, almost automatic. More on that later.

Now let's finish discussing why online job postings make a speed-run approach to networking necessary in the first place. Consider Becca's experience, for example (see sidebar, below). Online job postings are not inherently evil, nor was Becca being lazy by applying for so many jobs online—quite the opposite, actually. She was simply following the same old "mail and wait" paradigm her parents did, except electronically rather than with stamps and envelopes. It felt

The Resume Black Hole

I first met Becca (not her real name) in late March, a very high-stress time for many students. Campus recruiting has ended by then, so students without jobs at that point tend to panic. Their May graduation date is looming, and they realize that continuing to avoid the inherently rejection-heavy off-campus search is no longer an option.

Like most of her peers, Becca had assumed she would find her job while still on campus—she'd been at the top of her class her whole life, after all. But she hadn't found it, having underestimated the number and caliber of her competitors. She was so anxious that she canceled her spring break trip with a group of her classmates in order to focus on her job search. (Months later, she would call these spring break efforts a "garbage in, garbage out" job search.)

Becca spent her week off scanning job posting websites, hoping to find the perfect job. She was frustrated by the fact that all the interesting positions she found required candidates to have several years of previous relevant experience (which she lacked), but she hoped the strength of her resume would convince potential employers to give her a chance. In one last gasp on her last night of break, she spent eight consecutive hours surfing job postings and submitting resumes to dozens of employers.

She never heard back from a single one.

like progress, so she decided to invest as much time as she could into that approach rather than risk wasting time by experimenting with other approaches. This strategy is also known as *satisficing*. *Satisfice* is a hybrid word formed from *satisfy* and *suffice*. Coined by Nobel Prize–winning social scientist Herbert Simon in 1956, the term describes a person's tendency to select the first available solution that meets a given need rather than an optimal solution.

Believe it or not, satisficing is actually a good strategy in a majority of cases—it's what prevents us from spending hours deciding which of the dozens of hand soaps to buy at the grocery store. The alternative to satisficing is maximizing. *Maximizing* means finding the best possible choice, regardless of the amount of time or effort it takes. For major purchases like a house, erring on the side of maximizing rather than satisficing makes good sense, but in most cases satisficing, well, satisfices.

Hiring managers are classic satisficers, which makes total sense. Their ability to make outstanding hiring decisions rarely if ever factors into how big their raise is at the end of the year—therefore, they'll want to spend as little time making hiring decisions as possible. For them, finding a "good enough" candidate quickly is better than finding a "perfect" candidate slowly—so their hiring decision is very unlikely to involve reviewing hundreds of resumes!

The fundamental flaw in Becca's satisficing strategy was that she was satisficing on the wrong need; she satisficed on the *feeling* of making progress, rather than on actually making progress. To be fair, the latter is much more difficult and the route for how to do so is very unclear—thus many people make this error. But, unfortunately, just because something hurts doesn't make it exercise. I call this phenomenon the *Defensive Job Search* (DJS)—job searching for stats and validation rather than efficacy. The DJS is ubiquitous and hard to quit, but quitting it is an essential first step to a successful job search (see sidebar, page 6). No matter how diligently or efficiently Becca employed a defensive job search, pushing out resumes and cover letters to employers through online job postings, she was unlikely to succeed.

The Defensive Job Search

Keeping morale up during a job search is very difficult due to lack of positive reinforcement. The most important positive reinforcement—a job offer—comes at the very end of the process when it is no longer needed. Until then, the only sources of it are "Congratulations! Your application has been successfully submitted!" when succumbing to a job posting black hole, and "We know you're doing your best, honey" from your loved ones.

However, getting the latter often requires being able to quantify your effort in an understandable way. The two most accepted measures for doing so are (1) the number of online applications completed and (2) the number of hours spent searching through postings.

Unfortunately, neither of these correlates strongly with success. However, without knowing how to credibly achieve job search success, job seekers are being rational when they continue to pursue the achievable goal of affirmation, even if doing so is counterproductive to their actual goal.

This is the Defensive Job Search. In the DJS, job seekers prioritize visible efforts over results. Again, it is rational behavior, since the former is in your control and the latter is not. Scientists estimate that 70 percent of people feel what's called *Impostor Syndrome,* where we worry that others will find out we're not really as talented as they think we are.[2]

If you've ever felt Impostor Syndrome when job searching, please know that this uncertainty is not your fault. You have likely never been formally trained to job search—at least, not in the same way that you were trained in algebra or grammar. The good news is that a little bit of training goes a long way.

What I teach in this book is the opposite of the DJS. You will do very little applying online, and you'll only spend an hour or so strategically searching through job postings. Giving up these defensible *effort* metrics for *success* metrics (like your number of informational meetings, which we address in Part 3 of this book) may seem uncomfortable at first, but you'll soon be more productive and confident in your search—and your loved ones will soon learn to make that shift as well.

Technology in this case had, as Aldous Huxley said, only given job seekers a more efficient means for going backward. It simplified the application process to the point of ruin, drowning out the qualified candidates (who used to be willing to take the time and effort required to apply via the postal mail method, as they had good odds of success) among many unqualified candidates (who didn't bother to apply when the process was costly but applied in droves once those time and effort costs were removed). "Mail and wait" simply wasn't designed for the explosion in internet-aided applicants.

Technology also gave job search *expertise* a more efficient means for going backward. The struggle for clicks and views in a crowded job search–advice market incentivized output rather than curation, further overwhelming already-inundated job seekers with new books, articles, resources, and tips.

However, every additional piece of advice comes at a cost.

In his book *The Paradox of Choice*, psychologist Barry Schwartz discusses a study in which participants were allowed to select a free Godiva chocolate—some were allowed to choose from a box of six and others from a box of thirty. The surprising finding was that those who chose from the box of six were actually happier with their decision than those who had more to choose from. This can be attributed to a concept called *decision anxiety*.

When picking from a box of six chocolates, making the right choice is relatively easy—you either like nuts or you don't, you prefer dark chocolate to milk or white, and so on. However, in a box of thirty, you have only one-in-thirty odds of making the optimal choice. You may be tempted to examine each chocolate before making your choice (hopefully without touching them), losing time as well. You may even feel stressed after eating your chocolate, when you wonder whether you should have chosen differently. Similarly, a job seeker has to take time—sometimes just seconds and other times minutes or hours—to decide which articles to read and which approaches to implement. These distractions tax both our speed and our willpower.

Welcome to modern job searching! It is by far the single most important subject you were never taught in school.

I myself was blindsided by how poorly equipped I was for the modern job search, even after attending every workshop conducted by both my undergraduate *and* graduate career centers. Campus recruiting was consistently successful for me, leading me to my dream job in marketing. However, a few months into the job I'd spent my whole life planning for, my boss pulled me aside and told me, "Steve, marketing may not be the right career for you." I was devastated.

After the shock and denial wore off, I saw she was spot-on in her assessment. The job routinely minimized my strengths and accentuated my weaknesses, frustrating me so thoroughly that I dreaded the sound of my own alarm clock every morning. Since I no longer had access to campus recruiting, I decided to look online for an organizational plan that outlined how to conduct my very first "off-campus" job search. However, click after click, all I could find were laundry lists of tips rather than a coherent process. Even worse, the laundry lists tended to feature terrible clichés like "put yourself out there," "use your contacts," or "go to a local career fair" (adding irony to injury, since these largely disappeared with the advent of online job postings).

The reason I hate such careless advice is because—although it was delivered in optimistic and inspirational tones—it gave no consideration whatsoever to the limited amount of spare time and pain tolerance I actually had. As Barry Schwartz himself said in *The Paradox of Choice*, when we are given too many choices, "Choice no longer liberates. It debilitates. It might even be said to tyrannize." Even while unemployed, I wouldn't have the time to trial-and-error my way through all that advice, and even if *somehow* I did, following tips like "Wear a T-shirt that says 'Please Hire Me' into an interview" (actual advice I read) would save me the worry of ever being employed again.

That said, there is no way around the fact that the only way to get internal referrals is through networking. Personally, I *hate* networking. I find strangers intimidating, I'm terrible with names and worse with faces, and, believe it or not, I never learned how to be charming in my chemical engineering classes. However, I simply had to find a way to compensate for this limitation. I wanted instructions for doing that, not advice; but nothing of the sort seemed to exist. That is what I bring to you in this book, a process I've struggled daily to refine over two decades and thousands of iterations.

For the lucky minority of you who feel no anxiety at all about networking, know firstly that I'm incredibly jealous. Know secondly that you'll still get a lot of value from reading this book based on what I've heard from past 2HJS users in your camp. Taking a couple of hours to learn to structure, prioritize, and systemize your natural abilities will ensure you get the best possible outcome with the least possible effort.

Vivek (see sidebar, page 10) was correct in identifying the importance of creating personal relationships with recruiters, but he didn't use the technology available to him to diversify his efforts or manage his follow-up effectively, smothering those he sought to impress. Technologies like job search engines and social networking have unlocked a totally new, highly efficient way to job search, but it requires forgetting most of what you've learned before. "Mail and wait" as a strategy is obsolete, but so too is the concept of selling yourself.

The key to today's job search is a mix of high- and low-tech—specifically, using technology to efficiently locate a living, breathing advocate for you within your target employers. That is what this book will help you do. *Networking* is simply another way to say, "acquire internal referrals who will help get you job interviews"—and adding that bit of specificity to a vague yet critical concept makes it solvable.

2HJS works because it applies the Pareto principle to the job search, focusing on only what you need to know rather than on all the things you possibly could know. The Pareto principle, more commonly known as the 80/20 Rule, states that in most situations 80 percent of one's results can be attributed to 20 percent of one's actions. It is named for Italian economist Vilfredo Pareto, who noted in 1906 that 80 percent of Italy's land was owned by 20 percent of its population (and that 80 percent of his garden's peas came from 20 percent of his peapod plants, though that may just be urban legend). Interesting, but how does that concept get put to practical use?

The Low-Tech, Low-Tact Approach

Another student I worked with, whom I will call Vivek, had (unfortunately) come to my attention before we had even met—he had made waves among both his classmates and his recruiters for his aggressiveness.

Vivek wanted to become a strategy consultant with (and only with) an elite firm, and he was incredibly focused in his efforts. He would attend every event this handful of firms sponsored, meet every representative the companies sent, and unfailingly send them thank-you notes the next day. So far, so good.

Regrettably, although his networking skills in the moment were (mostly) correct, his overall strategy was not. Vivek was so desperate to sell himself that he ended up talking more than he listened, veering away from genuine relationship building into transparently transactional and quantity-based networking—a common mistake among those who focus on too small a universe of firms.

One of my former classmates—now a recruiter for one of those elite firms—called me after one of their events to catch up, and before hanging up, he gingerly asked me, "By the way, do you know Vivek?" Uh-oh.

Apparently, he had remembered Vivek monopolizing his time at their event and winced when he saw an informational meeting request from him a few days later. Informational meetings—or informational interviews—are conversations where people answer job seekers' questions and/or prescreen them for an interview; used correctly, informational meetings are also the most efficient way to acquire internal referrals. We cover them in detail in Part 3.

Just as my classmate feared he would, Vivek used that meeting to ask tedious questions like to those he had asked in person just a week before. This could have been forgivable had Vivek not also requested similar conversations on the same day with several other recruiters from that event.

As expected, Vivek did not get an offer from his top-choice firms—they found him well qualified but overzealous, making them uncomfortable about putting him in front of clients. Vivek was devastated and spent. He stopped job searching for nearly a month as he mentally recovered from watching his entire strategy collapse.

In the business world, it can be used to prioritize efforts. In 2002, Microsoft's then CEO Steve Ballmer acknowledged that 80 percent of crashes in Windows and Office were due to only 20 percent of the programs' bugs.[3] The programmers could have spread their time equally among all known issues in a quest for perfection (a maximizing approach). Alternatively, they could have addressed the easiest errors first to show quick results to investors and consumers (a satisficing approach). However, both of these strategies would have had less impact than their chosen path, which was to focus on the most disruptive 20 percent of issues first. Some of the less disruptive issues were likely never solved (surprising no Apple fans whatsoever) because entirely new versions of the software were soon released, rendering the remaining repairs unnecessary.

The job search is no different. There are immeasurable opportunities to be distracted by unnecessary details, and it takes discipline to stay focused. Most of my job seekers are so busy that they have only a couple of hours a week to devote to their search, so for them, achieving a high degree of efficiency is essential. 2HJS teaches readers a formal job search process that ensures they benefit from the 80/20 Rule at every step. It's not only for current students or first-time job seekers, either; it works for experienced professionals looking to change jobs midcareer, for military veterans transitioning into the civilian world, and for individuals who have been laid off or otherwise out of work no matter the length of time.

With all of the readily available information and technology, it's easier for job searchers to build relationships and identify targets. This process has *no* barriers to entry: it can be done just as well by someone without an advanced degree or a single LinkedIn contact as by one who has multitudes of each.

In its simplest form, the job search of today requires three distinct steps—*Prioritize*, *Contact*, and *Convince*—and each step gets its own in-depth treatment in this book. It is essential to Prioritize (Part 1) before embarking on a job search; otherwise, the infinite information available online becomes overwhelming and impossible to navigate. Once targets have been identified, you need to initiate

Contact (Part 2) before you can secure any advocacy. Once a sympathetic contact is listening, you can Convince (Part 3) them to be your ally. Consider Prioritizing and Contacting to be the tickets to launching your job search—these two steps will take up exactly two hours of your time. The next step, Convincing, is an ongoing investment that will vary with each employer, but helpful time estimates are provided.

In 2HJS, you'll know exactly what to do every single day once you wake up, and it will rarely amount to more than thirty minutes of effort. In fact, many days will require no job search effort whatsoever, giving you some well-deserved days off.

Lastly, it's important to note that this book is not a comprehensive job search guide. Such a book would be quite lengthy and mostly unnecessary—much like buying a travel guide to all of South America when you plan to visit only Peru. *This book's single-minded focus is to get you interviews as efficiently and quickly as possible.*

Taking a step back, here's a summary of the major steps of the job search process, and where this book fits in:

Choose what you want to do

Write a resume and cover letter

Prioritize target employers

Contact target employers

Convince advocates to provide
internal referrals

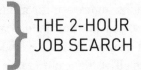

THE 2-HOUR
JOB SEARCH

Interview

Negotiate an offer

The 2HJS starts you at the point after you broadly identify what you want to do, and it ends once you secure formal interviews with your target employers. (For a similarly efficiency-minded approach to choosing a career, writing a resume, and developing interview skills, visit 2hourjobsearch.com to find more information on my follow-up book.)

Note that there is technology that I do *not* discuss in this book. There is no shortage of interesting job search technology out there, but that doesn't mean all of it is useful and/or necessary. 2HJS strives to be for "right-tech" rather than "high-tech," because cool isn't always helpful (and can often be quite the opposite). This book's mission isn't to impress you with all that technology can do—its mission is to help you harness well-established technology to make this process as pain-free, efficient, and effective as possible. Within two hours, starting from scratch, you will be done for the day—any further time would be unnecessary, but any less time would be insufficient. Thus, *The 2-Hour Job Search*.

Since 2008, I've taught this job search speedrunning process to every student who passes through Fuqua, but I recognize that not everyone has the means, desire, or opportunity to attend a major business school. That is why I consider my work developing and sharing the 2HJS job search process to be a moral obligation, since the vast majority of humanity's job searches are experienced far away from a university's friendly confines.

Similarly, while I originally built this process to help people seek jobs in business, it's proved useful to job seekers of all kinds, from programmers to engineers to creatives and beyond . . . with two notable exceptions: doctors and academics. While some elements of this book are still useful in those searches—for example, how to manage informational meetings—hiring decisions in these two areas tend to involve unique in-house processes and personalities. (For those of you pursuing roles in academia in particular, I highly recommend Karen Kelsky's *The Professor Is In*, which very much shares this book's ethos of bringing concrete structure to an inherently ambiguous process.)

Finally, after hundreds of iterations of teaching this material, I've found that my audiences frequently ask the same questions in a similar order each time. Therefore, each chapter is set up in a similarly ordered question-and-answer format to help you follow along and digest the material. The end of every chapter features a Troubleshooting section covering a few of the most commonly encountered challenges, along with instructions for navigating each one.

In terms of what you need on your end to follow my process, please make sure you have access to a spreadsheet software like

Microsoft Excel, an email program with an integrated calendar like Outlook or Gmail, and a LinkedIn profile (see sidebar, page 14).

I'm happy to say that both Becca's and Vivek's stories have happy endings. After working with me to learn how to execute his own 2-Hour Job Search, Vivek secured an internship with a boutique consulting firm; Becca received a full-time brand manager offer from a Midwestern food company. Becca's story didn't quite end there, however—through her 2HJS investigations, she came to realize that she found human resource management more appealing than pure marketing, so she declined her brand management offer. I asked her whether she wanted to meet me for help with restarting her search, and she told me, "Thank you, but I know what I'm doing now!" That comment *still* makes me smile.

LinkedIn Start-Up

LinkedIn is a (free) professional social networking site, and it proves very useful at various points in the 2-Hour Job Search. Create a profile now (you *will* need it later) by registering at LinkedIn.com and supplying basic objective information about your prior/current employers and education. Filling out your profile more completely than that (for example, with subjective descriptions of each position held) can take several hours, but that is not critical to this process and you can skip it until your outreach has been initiated.

To get started, search for your favorite (and/or most popular) coworker, boss, friend, and family member, and invite each of them to connect to you. This gives LinkedIn's technology an idea of who else is in your social network, and it will suggest people you may also want to connect to from there.

Once your initial contacts accept your invitation, their networks are notified that you've joined LinkedIn so that others will start reaching out to *you*. Thus, with no further effort of your own, your online network builds in the background. This gives you a great foundation for when we more actively engage LinkedIn in chapter 5.

#### PART 1

Prioritize: The LAMP List

LIST

 40 MINUTES

Quickstart Exercise #1

Identifying Dream Employers

Take the next sixty seconds and write down as many ideal employers as you can, particularly the ones that led you to read this book in the first place. Don't worry about whether these employers are logical or whether you're qualified to work for them—just worry about whether you'd actually accept a job from them in your field(s) of interest if one were offered to you.

If you are currently in school, write down employers that you wish had come to campus to recruit you.

Once this sixty seconds is up, set this list aside (note that it does not matter whether you wrote down two or ten employers—as long as you started a list, you succeeded). When we revisit this list shortly, it will give you a critical head start on the first step of the process.

And congratulations! Your 2-Hour Job Search experience is already under way!

What is a LAMP list?

The *LAMP list* (**L**ist, **A**dvocacy, **M**otivation, **P**osting) is a systematic and efficient seventy-minute process for making a prioritized list of target employers. Don't be intimidated, however, as no individual step takes longer than fifteen minutes to complete, making it easy to start and stop as time permits. The critical goal of the LAMP list is to end up with a prioritized, finite target list of at least forty employers that is precisely ordered based on three pieces of data that are both easy to find and predictive of success. The precise ordering is important so that you know exactly which target employers are best worth your spare time and energy at any given moment.

Why make a list? And why do I need so many employers in the list?

The list—of at least forty employers—is essential for moving beyond the "usual suspects," employers who tend to attract the most attention from job seekers (either in your local area or, if you're geographically flexible, more globally) and thus have the highest amount of competition and lowest odds of success. That's not to say the usual suspects are bad targets—they're great targets, especially given how highly motivating they often tend to be!—but fixating only on the usual suspects tends to turn out badly with remarkable predictability. Let's take a look at some national numbers for the US, keeping in mind that what's going on in the US nationally is also indicative of what's going on in your local region.

In 2018, there were 16 million businesses in the United States, and 165 million jobs were had between those employers. Of those jobs, nearly two-thirds were with employers with fewer than one hundred employees. Take a look for yourself:

EMPLOYER SIZE (# OF EMPLOYEES)	2018	
	BUSINESSES	JOBS
Total	16.0 million	164.9 million
Self-employed (1)	12.3%	1.2%
Stage 1 (2-9)	70.4%	26.2%
Stage 2 (10-99)	16.0%	36.4%
Stage 3 (100-499)	1.2%	19.8%
Stage 4 (500+)	0.1%	16.4%

Source: http://youreconomy.org/profile/index.lasso

Here it is in graphical terms:

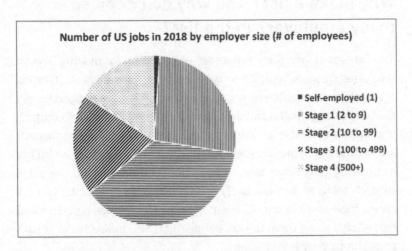

The Stage 3 and 4 employers may be the first ones that come to mind, but they make up just 1.3 percent of available employers, and between them, they account for just over one-third of all employment in the US. The remaining 98.7 percent of employers offer paychecks just like the largest 1.3 percent do, but too often I see job seekers either ignore them or refuse to consider them because their names are unfamiliar, effectively eliminating two-thirds of available job opportunities without a second (or really even a first) thought.

Furthermore, that 98.7 percent of employers are the ones with the least competition for spots simply because they do *not* have household names. In most cases, Stage 1 and 2 employers would be quite happy with "good enough" talent who are proactive and make it easy for the employer to hire them—this *especially* includes job seekers who lack directly relevant work experience, ideal work references, or a steady timeline of work over the years.

Because there are now databases that allow job seekers to find these sixteen million employers, it is more important than ever to identify a subset that is of particular interest before you begin in order to avoid being overwhelmed by the possibilities.

On the flip side, if your search is geographically restricted, it's tempting to focus on "the only employers in town." However, note that no town has a single employer—not even Bentonville, Arkansas (home of megacorporation Walmart), nor Los Alamos, New Mexico (where 38 percent of the city's 12,000 residents work for the Los Alamos National Laboratory).[1] Other employers must spring up to support these organizations.

Granted, if you're a nurse and there is only one hospital in the area (a regrettable market situation that economists call *monopsony*—in monopolies there is only one seller of a good or service, but in monopsonies there is only one buyer), this may involve either leaving your profession (temporarily or otherwise), starting your own business, or a reluctant move to a city with more opportunities. None are ideal options, but in limited-geography situations it is even more important to identify your alternatives before beginning your search, since in-town lower wage roles can actually result in a higher net income and overall life satisfaction than professional roles that require hours-long commutes each way.

(Note: Regardless of whether your search is local or remote most informational meetings conducted using 2HJS will be by phone since many contacts will prefer this to meeting in-person with a stranger. So, whether your job search is local or countrywide, the technology you use will be the same!)

By creating a list of employers, we are essentially drawing the borders of our job search, taking an intimidating and infinite-seeming job search universe and turning it into something pleasantly finite; this makes filling in the three LAMP list data points for those employers a self-contained, minimally stressful activity, just like coloring the pictures in a coloring book.

A good example of how making a list of target employers is effective can be found in an unlikely source: reality television. On ABC's *The Bachelor*, twenty-five women are isolated in a house and given a chance to form a relationship with one eligible bachelor. Based on the Bachelor's preferences, one or more women are eliminated each episode until only one winner remains, and voilà, romance blossoms for a couple of weeks. (The genders are reversed in the show's equally salacious spinoff, *The Bachelorette*; we'll stick to *The Bachelor* in this discussion for simplicity.)

Watching this show physically pains me—I have a very low tolerance for awkwardness, which for a career coach is like being a doctor with a latex allergy—but I've always found its game theory fascinating. Who *wouldn't* be a good Bachelor if you limited supply and maximized demand like that? I mean, the guy has a 100 percent chance of winning; his entire strategy consists of "Get my own TV show."

On the flip side, being a female contestant on *The Bachelor* is an awful proposition. Supply is artificially restricted, and demand is artificially inflated. Each woman has just one-in-twenty-five odds of winning, and she also forgoes a month or so of normal dating activity (and perhaps a job as well) in order to play—and she hasn't even seen the guy! It's dehumanizing and a long shot at best, so who would do such a thing?

Sadly, every year I see dozens of very smart people do exactly this—voluntarily subject themselves to situations with high competition and low odds of success (in the form of online job postings), desperately hoping someone gives them a chance.

There are numerous downsides to this approach, but the worst of all is the toll it takes on one's confidence. I have seen people who've lived their whole lives at the top of their class be shaken by the epic silence after submitting to an online job posting to the point where they'd be willing to accept *anything* just to make the anxiety stop.

This is *not* an attractive look to employers. Shocking, right? Employers are excellent at detecting which candidates have other active prospects and which do not—many will even ask directly during interviews where else job seekers are interviewing—and they have a strong preference for those with richer prospects. They assume that how a job seeker approaches their job *search* is predictive of how they'll approach their *job*: is this the type of candidate who puts all their eggs in one basket and hopes their lack of contingency planning will never come to light, or is this the type of candidate who creates a strategy and backup plans for if (really, when) events don't go as planned? If you were the interviewer, which kind of candidate would *you* prefer to hire?

There's a certain confidence and serenity that accompanies job seekers who have other options in process when they speak with an employer—they don't need any single interview to work out since they have other prospects waiting in the wings. But for the latter group those attributes are impossible to simulate; a desperate job seeker really needs every single interview to work out since there are usually no others on the horizon to take the pressure off. Those job seekers essentially go from one season of *The Bachelor* to the next, starting from scratch each time an opportunity doesn't work out.

Wouldn't an employer prefer a candidate who considers them their "dream employer," though?

Yes, of course! Just not at the expense of practicality. Identifying a dream employer is not a valid excuse for shunning all others. Furthermore—and this is a common theme throughout the book—*you can't control outcomes; you can only control process.*

Good process yields good outcomes, yes. However, because you never make the final hiring decision, there is simply no way to guarantee a positive outcome, just like there is no way to guarantee any single coin flip comes up tails and no way for a contestant to ensure the Bachelor picks *her*.

So, what can we do about it?

Let's stick with *The Bachelor* analogy a bit longer. In game theory terms, a contestant could employ two methods to improve her chance of "winning": increase the odds of the game (say, finding a dating show on which only ten women compete rather than twenty-five) or increase the number of times the game can be played. An even better approach, however, is to become the Bachelor himself: collect a large number of preliminary candidates, narrow them down by collecting key pieces of information about each one, and focus primarily on the strongest prospects. That is effectively what the LAMP list does for job seekers.

Why make a LAMP list, specifically?

The LAMP list allows for efficient gathering of specific, useful employer information, providing black-and-white data for choosing which employers to approach and in what order.

LAMP guarantees efficiency in two main ways: it ensures that similar tasks are grouped together to save time and that each task is carried out with the appropriate level of detail—and no more. It accomplishes this by limiting research to three pieces of data that are easy to find and predictive of success: namely, Advocacy, Motivation, and Posting. These factors are proxies for "perfect" pieces of information (we discuss this in more detail in chapter 2), and they are later used to prioritize your target employers so you approach the most important and time-sensitive ones first. In short, LAMP uses the 80/20 Rule to get 80 percent of the benefit of employer research in 20 percent of the time. Heeding the words of Voltaire, we do not allow the perfect to be the enemy of the good.

In this chapter, we discuss how to create a robust List (the "L" in LAMP) of potential target employers, and in the subsequent chapters in Part 1 we examine how to quickly find information about **A**dvocacy, **M**otivation, and **P**osting. At that point, our LAMP list will be completely filled in, but we will need to properly sort it to complete the Prioritize step of 2HJS's titular two-hour "launch sequence." Thus Part 1 of this book (that is, the time required to complete the tasks covered in each chapter) looks like this:

CHAPTER #	TIME REQUIRED
Chapter 1: **L**ist column	40 minutes
Chapter 2: **A**dvocacy column	10 minutes
Chapter 3: **M**otivation column	5 minutes
Chapter 4: **P**osting column	15 minutes
Total for Part 1: Prioritize	70 minutes

There will be great temptation during the LAMP process to cheat—for example, to pause your LAMP list-making efforts in order to quickly apply to an interesting job posting—but if you give in, you've lost your efficiency.

Won't applying to an online job only take fifteen minutes?

Occasionally, yes, but once you factor in reading the job description, filling out your personal information, confirming your email address, uploading a resume—or, worse, converting your resume information into their custom format—and answering whatever screening questions they pose to you, it usually takes much, much longer.

But for argument's sake, let's say every online job posting takes only fifteen minutes to complete. The problem is that it takes fifteen minutes *every time* . . . and a shred of your soul; and you only have a finite supply of time and shreds of soul to throw at this process. Online job postings are the worst place to throw them.

But what if the posting closes before I can apply?

This is a fair question. However, outside of government jobs (and job postings from your school's internal jobs portal if you're a current student), I can assure you that I've never seen the "ticking time bomb" scenario actually happen—one where you make a new advocate at a target employer with an open position, only to hear, "You'd be a great fit, but because you didn't get your online application in on time we can't consider you." Employers always make exceptions for internal referrals because a current employee is willing to risk their own social capital to advocate for you, demonstrating how strongly that employee thinks you should be considered. That risk is what makes referrals so powerful.

Furthermore, think about the last online job posting to which you applied for a job you genuinely wanted. In fact, think of the last ten. Did you get an interview from those applications? If so, by all means keep applying—there is something in your background that is getting attention, which eludes nearly everyone else who submitted their resume. Similarly, if you work in a job function that is in high demand—to the point where you are regularly approached by recruiters about open positions in your desired line of work—you may want to get a different book!

However, if you did not get any response, don't worry about applying to every single job posting you see, because it's a terrible use of effort; and, as you've seen, it's not leading to interviews anyway.

In this book, we simply take a fraction of that time you would have spent agonizing over online job applications that were unlikely to yield interviews and instead funnel it into having conversations with experts in your desired field, making you smarter and improving your odds with each one. By contrast, online job posting applications are more like lottery tickets—they have a cost, they are *very* unlikely to be winners, and losing yesterday in no way improves your odds of winning today.

That said, the existence of exciting online job postings does factor in to how we create and prioritize our LAMP list, but we'll cover that in chapter 4.

In summary, let bad job seekers get distracted by the online job posting black hole—their distraction will make your job search that much easier. Also, know that following LAMP's steps correctly will get you back to any intriguing opportunities within two hours.

So how long should this target employer list be?

Forty employers.

Forty?! Can I start with fewer than forty employers?

You could, but I've never seen anyone be successful in the process who has done so. If you start with fewer than forty employers, you are in fact *not* following 2HJS. You might be doing a search that shares some similarities with 2HJS, but all the pieces of this process are designed to work together in a very specific way.

2HJS is an attrition-based job search strategy, meaning that most of the employers you start the process with will be eliminated (or, more accurately, deprioritized) along the way. In the sorting stage of LAMP (chapter 4), employers are deprioritized because they are of lower interest and/or do not offer as many positive indicators of employment. Starting with fewer than forty employers results in a weaker target list that usually skews toward obvious, high-profile organizations that tend to draw a lot of competition for open spots, resulting in a longer, more difficult job search and less leverage when a match is found.

That being said, while we are brainstorming forty employers, if you follow the 2HJS process correctly, you will not actually contact more than ten of them before you find a job. You do, however, have to identify forty in order to narrow it down to the right ten—there's simply no way to shortcut the diverge-then-converge nature of this process and still be successful, and forty has durably proved to be the magic minimum number for an effective LAMP list.

So, if forty employers is good, is more than forty better?

Absolutely, the more the merrier, provided you can do so within the time limits provided and do not exceed one hundred!

It costs negligible additional time to add possible employers at this point of the process, just as it does to send more units through an assembly line that's already up and running. Exception handling is what takes most of your time. Thus, if you find a resource that with minimal effort can give you twenty more potential employers when you're already sitting on thirty, copy in all twenty—do not artificially end your list at number forty and do not research all twenty to pick out your favorite ten!

I've seen functional LAMP lists with up to one hundred employers. However, any more than that and the list gets a bit unwieldy. Finding our three data points takes longer for one hundred employers than for forty, so aim for a happy medium within that range, knowing that most 2HJS users come in at or just above forty.

In my experience, those job seekers who don't expand their consideration set beyond the first handful of employers that immediately come to mind often fail to find a job with any of them, leading to a period of depression and a suspension of effort lasting weeks or even months before the job seeker can muster the energy to start over.

This is why all full-time MBA students at Duke University must create a LAMP list with at least forty "custom" employers (so called because they are chosen according to each student's own interests) who don't already recruit on campus, and use 2HJS to initiate contact with their Top 5 in order to participate in campus interviews (which nearly all wish to do). Not only does this help our career center fulfill our ethical obligation to our students to prepare them for life after we're gone, but it also improves their odds of finding a meaningful job faster by giving them options outside of the convenient ones that come to campus—and thus automatically have high competition.

Now, some of my students have shown me lists of twenty custom employers, swearing there were absolutely no other employers out there to consider. However, not only is that patently false, but also it's self-defeating. A twenty-employer list doesn't go far enough to force genuine creativity and help people find the right job.

A job seeker can get to twenty without making *any* concessions on location, brand recognition, job function, industry, and the like. However, getting to forty means struggling with the question, "What ideal job element am I willing to concede first?" That doesn't mean giving up any of your ideals during the search itself (unless you are seeking something ultraspecific, like becoming an art buyer for the Smithsonian Institution), but it does mean beginning to prioritize instead of just hoping for an ideal fit. Again, employers want to hire people who make contingency plans, not ones who consider "hope for the best" a strategy.

Furthermore, the best careers (and easiest job searches) are rarely found through 100 percent rational or linear thought. In my experience, those who find the job search process least stressful are the ones who combine their aptitudes with their passions. Why is that? Two main reasons:

1. They genuinely enjoy learning about the employers to whom they speak rather than seeing such conversations as just a means to an end. One of my most motivated job-seeking students, Adam, had been an IT consultant before business school, and he desperately wanted to break into the mobile phone industry despite not having a relevant background. He just adored following the industry. He hit the pavement and truly enjoyed talking to the contacts he made at the major firms, but none had any jobs for him. Still, his efforts paid off. How?

2. They experience less competition when they target nonobvious employers. For Adam, a contact at the fourth mobile phone company he spoke to (which didn't have a job for him) recommended he talk to a colleague of his at the organization

that sets standards across all mobile phone manufacturers to ensure compatibility. He did so, and the first question they asked him was, "What do you know about the mobile phone industry?" Bingo.

Because of his prior conversations using the 2HJS process for informational meetings, Adam was easily able to discuss the major trends impacting the industry, the challenges the current market leaders were facing, and where he thought the new technology was headed. They offered him a job the next day. When you have knowledge, people want to hire you. When you have both passion and knowledge, people want to hire you *immediately*.

What if I haven't identified a passion?

That's totally fine! Personal passions don't have to be the centerpiece of every job you ever have. In fact, some job seekers purposely postpone a more enjoyable career to accomplish other personal or professional goals first—working for a while as an investment banker is a great way to earn seed money for your future start-up company or career in a nonprofit organization, for example, and working in IT is a great way to provide for your family while saving up for physical therapy grad school. Moreover, the process of discovering your passions is iterative—you have to kiss a lot of possible passion frogs before you find your prince. (For proof, please see my previous chemical engineering, strategy consulting, and marketing careers!) Consider each iteration of your LAMP list as bringing you one step closer to finding *the* career you'll want to dedicate your life to.

I just want to make sure you have applied some creativity *before* deciding whether your current-moment dream employer is "the one." This comes from a body of research called *temporal construal theory*, which states that people tend to make *higher-order* (i.e., better) decisions in advance than we do in the heat of the moment—such as deciding ahead of time to order a salad at dinner because you're trying to watch your waistline (a longer-term health and appearance consideration) rather than ordering whatever looks best after reviewing the menu (a fleeting taste consideration). We revisit temporal construal theory in chapter 7.

Compelling students to complete a list of forty possible employers accomplishes this nearly every time. I've seen this simple act liberate students mentally to the point where they admit their initial career search focus—those first five to ten employers—was more of a family or peer expectation than a personal desire, and they decide to shift their job search focus ahead to that "future" career immediately. Powerful stuff.

A more unconscious process takes over when job seekers are pushed beyond the obvious choices. What websites do they check for ideas? Which articles catch their attention? How do they spend their weekends, for that matter? Those personal default inclinations and interests are really where exceptional and fulfilling careers lie. Optimal career selection is not the main focus of this book, but it is one further benefit in addition to increased job search efficiency and reduced stress. (Note: If you are struggling to identify *any* careers of interest, my favorite method for attempting to fast-track that process is the Odyssey Plans exercise from Dave Evans and Bill Burnett's excellent book, *Designing Your Life*.)

Finally, a large target list encourages job seekers to consider smaller employers. As we learned earlier, 99 percent of employers have fewer than one hundred employees, yet that other 1 percent of employers tends to capture our attention most of the time, making us feel that they are the only options available. They certainly are not, so you should not rule out employers with whom you are simply unfamiliar during this list-making exercise.

A contestant from *The Bachelor* could dramatically increase her odds of finding a mate by dating in non-TV venues; she could then be considered on her own merits instead of vis-à-vis twenty-four competitors. Similarly, lesser-known employers will attract less competition, increasing the odds that you are considered on your own merits, not relative to hundreds of other applicants.

Most of those employers you're unfamiliar with will likely never need to be researched further in the 2HJS because they won't display any positive indicators of likely job search success. However, some will give you a compelling reason to research them later—a relevant job posting, for example. It costs very little time to include additional employers (both well known and unknown) early in the process, but trying to add them later is very time consuming.

For real, though—what if I can't list any dream employers because I have no idea what I want to do?

I got you. See the sidebar.

What do I need to do to get started?

Open a blank spreadsheet in Microsoft Excel or Google Sheets. In the top row, label your first four columns "List," "Advocacy," "Motivation," and "Posting." (You may also download a blank preformatted LAMP list from www.2hourjobsearch.com.) That's really it. Note that in this chapter, we will only be filling in the first column, List (which I will often refer to as the *L column*).

So how do I do this within forty minutes?

There is an old proverb that asks, "How does a man eat an elephant?" The answer is, "One bite at a time." Anything is possible—even a seemingly overwhelming situation—if you develop the ability to break the project into small, manageable pieces.

If you find yourself getting distracted (checking your phone, surfing the internet, and so on), know that this is totally natural and the process will take some getting used to. Simply (and without judgment) acknowledge that your focus has drifted, take a deep breath, and return to the 2HJS task at hand.

Theoretically, LAMP users may generate their forty-employer list in an infinite number of ways, but in my experience, targeting the following four groups has proved most effective for getting this done

Addressing the BIG Question—What Should I Do with My Life?

If you're struggling with this anxiety, know that the first step is to *relax*. Very few people know what their passions are, and thus many struggle to figure out what to do with their lives. A vast majority of my business students—whose ages typically range from their mid-twenties to early thirties—go to graduate school specifically so they can change careers!

I've worked with job seekers in their forties and fifties about making similar changes, and it all boils down to the same common challenge—finding a way to combine your strengths with your passions (or at least your interests in the interim until you've figured out what your passions actually are).

Of the two, your strengths are certainly easier to assess. What have been your proudest moments professionally up to this point? Why were they so, and what unique skill or blend of skills was required to pull it off? Here's a more engaging way to consider this question: if your life depended on naming a skill at which you think you're in the top 1 percent of the world, what would it be? (This is a very hard question for most people, by the way—but it often is challenging enough to get job seekers thinking the right way.)

For further reading on this topic, I strongly recommend *StrengthsFinder 2.0* by Tom Rath. It will help you identify your top five strengths (among a possible thirty-four) and understand how they uniquely interact to make you "you" in an ownable rather than clichéd way.

Assessing passions can be more difficult, however. If you don't have time to read books on self-assessment, pick up the latest issue of the *New York Times* and mark the articles you're most interested in reading. Don't actually read them—simply flag them and keep looking. After you've found a few that have caught your eye, determine what those articles have in common. (This approach is referred to more broadly as a *bright spot analysis*. We use it again shortly!)

That said, not everyone has found their passions yet. Don't try to force it, or even worse, try to equate hobbies with passions (that's simply a fast route to hating your hobbies). If you don't have an identifiable passion, tapping into your interests in the interim will totally suffice.

continued

Think back to what topics you've learned the most about over the past year. Your intrinsic desire for improvement is far more important than your existing knowledge in the advocacy-based search 2HJS involves, so pick a subject you'd like to immerse further in and start there, knowing you can always switch focus later if you find that subject isn't as engaging as you'd hoped.

I'll close this answer with one more concept from Evans and Burnett's *Designing Your Life*: there is no single "best possible life." There are many great lives to be lived—it's just a matter of choosing which one(s) to pursue first. Therefore, take the pressure off yourself to get this one "right." All answers are correct, and all will make you better prepared for your next iteration.

in forty minutes: (1) dream employers, (2) alumni (or affinity) employers, (3) actively hiring employers, and (4) trending employers. For the best results, I ask my job seekers for "ten employers or ten minutes"—whichever comes first—for each of the four groups to approach:

GROUP	BENEFITS	BEST FOR JOB SEEKERS WHO ARE . . .
(1) Dream employers	Intuitive; research is applicable to multiple employers	• Targeting a specific industry, sector, or location
(2) Alumni (or affinity) employers	Have contacts at every target employer	• Targeting a specific role/job title or location • Undecided about their career • Shy
(3) Actively hiring employers	Target employers are currently hiring	• Targeting a specific role/job title or location
(4) Trending employers	Learn about industry while researching; locate less obvious employers	• Switching careers • Seeking smaller employers

As a reminder, not all employers your research uncovers will be well known, but you should include any that match your search criteria in your LAMP list at this point in the process. Those that are neither familiar to you nor offer hope for employment are quickly screened out later—you just won't know which those are until after your LAMP list is completed.

APPROACH #1: DREAM EMPLOYERS

The "dream employers" approach consists of first adding the employers you have always aspired to work for in your spreadsheet's L column and then systematically looking up each employer's peers and adding them in your L column as well.

The good news is that you have already started this process! Bring out that list of employers you created in Quickstart Exercise #1 at the very start of this chapter—these are your first entries in your L column. (Note: If you skipped Quickstart Exercise #1, I get it—but seriously, take sixty seconds right now and do a brain dump of every employer you can immediately think of that you'd really like to work for before we proceed with our brainstorm; it genuinely makes this whole process both easier and more effective.)

This approach tends to work best for readers targeting a particular sector, because any research done on one employer will likely apply to their competitors as well. If you came up with more than five employers in Quickstart Exercise #1, it generally means you have a sector, industry, or location in mind. In that case, Google a list of companies in that sector, industry, or location and the lists that come up will help you get to ten (and beyond) in ten minutes pretty easily.

That said, if you struggled to come up with at least three employers in Quickstart Exercise #1, it generally indicates you don't have a particular industry or set of industries in mind. If that is the case, this is totally fine and frankly very common! My favorite technique for breaking this form of writer's block is detailed in Technology Corner #1 on page 34.

There are database services that can help you research potential employers, but they often charge fees for usage, require a login to be accessed, or otherwise slow you down, so whenever possible, I recommend sticking to free resources like Google and Wikipedia during this ten-minute step (by looking up, for example, "list of companies in Battle Creek, Michigan" or "socially conscious apparel companies").

Identifying "People Also Viewed" Employers

Periodically in this book, I share with you free technologies that help you get this process done as efficiently as possible. To ensure you always have access to the latest and greatest technology recommendations for completing the 2HJS process, please join the book's free LinkedIn Group called "The 2-Hour Job Search—Q&A Forum."

LinkedIn's People Also Viewed box helps job seekers apply the bright spot analysis when they can only identify one or two initial employers of interest.

To access the People Also Viewed box, enter one of your "dream employers" in LinkedIn's main search box and click on their Company page. Scroll down, and to the right you'll see a People Also Viewed section listing five related employers that other LinkedIn users looked up. These tend to be direct competitors of your dream employer, or at worst they're in the same general industries and/or locations. If you see some you like, add them to your list! If you see some you don't know well, add them to your list (remember, you don't rule out employers just because you've never heard of them).

If you see one that looks particularly good, click on that employer's name. This opens up a new employer page, which has its own, slightly different People Also Viewed list, and so on, providing an almost Tinder-like interface where you can react to the names LinkedIn puts in front of you.

This technique works best for smaller employers rather than large ones; looking up one of the Big Five tech firms inevitably brings up the other four, for example, so think small in this case.

Screen-Hopping

Periodically in this book, I share with you common and/or costly mistakes previous users of 2HJS have made; I present these in Time Out sidebars like this one.

Switching between maximized computer applications (what I call screen-hopping) can be a time-consuming process—you effectively lose your momentum and train of thought every time you switch from your web browser to your spreadsheet.

An easy way to improve your efficiency is to split your screen. If you have multiple monitors, put your LAMP list on one and your web browser on the other. If you do most of your work on a laptop, narrow your LAMP list spreadsheet to show just the L column, and move it to the far right side of your browser so it covers only a quarter of your screen at most. Your web browser should take up the remaining three-quarters on the left side of the screen.

This way, you don't have to lose your place and reorient whenever you find an employer to add to your LAMP list. Arranging your screen this way now instead of screen-hopping can save you significant time and energy by not needlessly taxing your memory, concentration, and patience!

Why is the dream employer approach effective?

The reason the dream employer approach works so well is its use of the aforementioned 80/20 Rule—the competitor lists are not comprehensive or perfectly relevant, but they are easy to access quickly, and ruling employers out still helps put you in the mind-set of the Bachelor rather than one of the twenty-five contestants.

You may be *very* tempted to research the unfamiliar employers you find as you go, but resist that urge. Your progress will slow dramatically if tasks are blended, since you'll be introducing a second goal into what was a straightforward single-goal process. It's impossible to search for *and* research employers at the same time; what you'd really be doing is switching back and forth between searching and researching. Every switch requires two mental steps from a cognitive perspective—goal shifting and rule activation—and each one exacts a toll in terms of efficiency and effort.

Thus, when you try to search and research simultaneously, you're moving from a simple copy-and-paste operation requiring little thought to a complicated activity with multiple simultaneous goals and scores of small decisions. "Should I click on that link? Should I read that job description?" Each decision and sidetrack may take only a few seconds and a bit of effort, but those costs add up quickly.

Remember that our goal is to brainstorm at least ten new employers within ten minutes for each of the four approaches we'll use to fill in our L column. This is just the first of those four brainstorming methods, so if you are struggling with this one, don't worry! We've got three more groups yet to try, any of which can help you get to forty employers.

At this point an example may be helpful.

A computer programmer interested in breaking into the crowd-funding space might Google "list of crowdfunding companies" and end up with an L column that looks like this:

#	LIST	ADVOCACY	MOTIVATION	POSTING
1	Kickstarter			
2	Indiegogo			
3	Patreon			
4	GoFundMe			
5	Network for Good			
6	Classy			
7	Crowdfunder			
8	GiveGab			
9	Razoo			
10	Funraise			

Note that it's very unlikely the computer programmer has heard of every single one of these companies. In fact, it's possible the job seeker *never* learns more about these unfamiliar companies in their 2HJS process. Even then, they have still served their purpose. They have expanded that job seeker's consideration set beyond the obvious candidates like Kickstarter, providing the job seeker additional opportunities to both learn from experts in the crowdfunding field and gain advocacy within that space.

Finally, while I encourage you to find at least ten employers in this ten-minute span of time, don't spin your wheels if you can't. Just move on to the next method.

Oh, and just like that, you earn your first check mark!

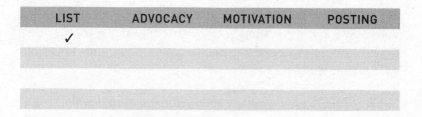

LIST	ADVOCACY	MOTIVATION	POSTING
✓			

That's one down, three to go.

APPROACH #2: ALUMNI (OR AFFINITY) EMPLOYERS

This approach consists of identifying organizations that currently employ people like you. These employers have some understanding of the value you can bring to their organization, and you are also more likely to be able to develop an advocate within that organization, given your shared backgrounds.

For some job seekers, this means looking up alumni of your most recent college or university. While many schools provide alumni with access to an alumni database, I actually prefer going straight to LinkedIn's custom search interface (see Technology Corner #2, page 39) to look up this information. Most professionals are intrinsically motivated to update their employer information on LinkedIn but generally require reminders and cajoling from their alma maters to update their schools' alumni databases directly.

In LinkedIn's custom search interface, just enter your most recent school into the Education search field and look through the organizations that are currently employing other graduates of your program for ideas. If you have attended a graduate school, enter that specific graduate school (rather than the university more broadly), as it will be more densely populated with relevant alumni rather than with a mix of all professions.

If your search returns too many results, enter a relevant keyword (like "realtor" or "programmer") into the Job Title search field and repeat your search.

This approach also works very well for those targeting a specific city or state. Just enter your geographic constraints (for example, "San Francisco"), and if any alum has an interesting employer or job title, copy the employer's name (but not the alum's! Keep your focus!) into your list and move on.

What if I don't have many (or any) alumni connections?

For job seekers without access to university alumni connections—such as high school or technical school graduates, those graduating from smaller colleges or programs, or those transitioning from the military—substitute an affinity population for a literal alumni population. The single best method for doing this is through another free LinkedIn tool, LinkedIn Groups.

What are LinkedIn Groups?

LinkedIn Groups are self-selecting affinity groups within LinkedIn. They are *the* best-kept secret in the modern job search, offering nearly immediate networks and learning opportunities from like-minded individuals (just as this book's LinkedIn Group provides a platform for discussing how best to use the 2HJS process). LinkedIn Groups are valuable to all job seekers, but they are particularly important to those without alumni populations, as they provide a lot of the benefits of an alumni network without the exorbitant tuition costs.

Custom Searching in LinkedIn

LinkedIn can offer an overwhelming number of features, especially for novice users. However, there is no need to become a LinkedIn expert in order to do the 2HJS process. Quite the contrary, there are just a few features you'll need to learn. Custom searching in LinkedIn is perhaps the most important.

Custom searching offers you the ability to specify multiple criteria (such as current employer, schools attended, location, and much more) so you can find who you're looking for faster and more accurately. However, finding it isn't entirely straightforward, so here are some instructions to help.

As of this printing, the easiest way to call up the custom search screen is to simply click on the search box at the top of the screen when you log into LinkedIn and click Enter without typing anything. That brings up a search ribbon at the top of the screen with a button called All Filters. Click on that button, and that brings you to the custom search interface.

You have to request to join LinkedIn Groups, but if and when you are approved, you can see what discussions are top of mind for others in your desired areas or who share your background, either by checking the group regularly online or asking for a digest of discussions to be sent to you regularly.

More importantly, once accepted into the group, you can access a directory of fellow members. For example, by opening the directory for a military veterans LinkedIn Group, you can see not just which companies employ fellow veterans but also what sorts of jobs they are hired to do, helping you further identify possible careers you may want to pursue.

Join a combination of large and small groups. Larger groups give you access to many like-minded people (which will be very helpful when we begin our outreach in Part 2 of 2HJS, Contact) and more robust discussions of current events, while smaller, more targeted groups are especially helpful immediately, as they offer you the most curated set of relevant employers.

Is there any disadvantage to using advocates through LinkedIn Groups for this brainstorm?

There is one disadvantage, and that is an inability to do a filtered search (by location, job title, or industry, for example) within a LinkedIn Group, as you can using LinkedIn's custom search screen. Still, it's a minor inconvenience in the grand scheme of this process, as this is only one of four brainstorming techniques for you to use.

Therefore, if you find LinkedIn Groups too inconvenient (or too inaccessible, if you have not yet been granted access to any relevant groups) as a brainstorming tool and you do not have ready access to a population of relevant alumni or advocates elsewhere, feel free to swap this method out for an additional ten minutes and ten employers spent identifying dream employers using our previous method.

Why is the alumni/affinity employer approach effective?

This method is effective because it is reactive rather than proactive. In the dream employer group, you have to proactively have an idea in mind to seek out, but in this method, you can browse what is available instead. For job seekers uncertain of what career they would like to pursue next, any open-ended search (for example, by a particular city or industry) will generate a list of professionals with very different job titles at a wide assortment of organizations. Some jobs will seem more appealing than others, and identifying a few specific job titles of interest will greatly simplify your search, both now and later in the 2HJS process.

Another benefit of this brainstorming approach is that, if you're shy about approaching strangers, the only employers you find will be ones where you have a shared school or affinity group connection with at least one of the employees there. (Note that by the end of 2HJS, you'll be comfortable reaching out to just about anyone whose career path interests you—alumni, advocate, or total stranger—but we'll get to that later. First things first!)

As with our dream employer method, simply copy any employer name that looks like it could be interesting from your browsing activity into your LAMP list and keep going. Remember that the goal is ten employers in ten minutes for each of our four brainstorming methods (of which this is our second), so don't worry about being perfect or comprehensive—err on the side of including employers who meet your basic criteria even if they are currently unfamiliar to you.

As a reminder again to stay true to the LAMP process, it is important *not* to copy and paste alumni/advocate contact information (for example, names or job titles) during this step. It may seem efficient to capture that data at this time, but that's wrong for two main reasons. First, capturing that data now involves switching applications—for example, from your web browser to your spreadsheet and back—many, many times. Each copy and paste may take just thirty seconds, but those seconds add up fast, and each represents a chance for getting distracted and losing your train of thought (especially if you are screen-hopping as outlined in Time Out #1 on page 35). Second, you most likely only need contact information for up to ten of your possible target employers, so gathering contacts for all forty targets involves a lot of unnecessary effort.

A singular focus is what makes each LAMP step so fast, and in this step, you are simply listing possible employers.

And with that, you get your second check mark.

LIST	ADVOCACY	MOTIVATION	POSTING
✓			
✓			

APPROACH #3: ACTIVELY HIRING EMPLOYERS

This approach consists of looking up job postings in an online job search engine and adding potential employers that are actively advertising desirable positions. Job search engines (I tend to use

Advocacy Now, Advocacy Later

Highlight employers you found using the alumni/affinity approach with a colored font or background in your L column—doing so now will save you time later when we fill in our Advocacy column after our L column is completed.

Indeed.com most frequently) are websites that allow users to use a search engine interface to simultaneously search many other websites for relevant job postings.

Why is the actively hiring employer approach effective?

The key advantage to this approach is that it limits results to just those companies that are currently hiring. It also enjoys one of the same benefits as the alumni brainstorming approach in that it easily performs searches that are restricted to a specific geography or function (for example, marketing or computer programming). It's also simple to use—Indeed.com specifically asks for only two inputs: "What" and "Where." For "What," you input keywords (like your most recent degree, if relevant) or job titles of interest (like "chemical engineer" or "office manager"). For "Where," you enter specific cities, zip codes, or states of interest, if desired. (If you are searching multiple roles or cities, simply divide your ten minutes among searches for each role or city you're targeting, entering the employers you find in a single shared L column—we discuss how to account for these varied options when we sort our LAMP list in chapter 4.)

After that, click on Find Jobs or press Enter, and within seconds you have a list of possible employers you can add to your LAMP list. (Note that you're not even paying attention to the age of these job postings, since your singular focus for this ten minutes is identifying organizations that employ people like you in your desired role or city. We account for posting age and relevance in chapter 4.)

However, this approach also presents a LAMP user's single biggest risk of inefficiency. It can be awfully tempting to click on interesting-looking postings for more info, rather than just copying and pasting the employers' names into your LAMP list per the instructions. DO NOT DO THIS. This is akin to taking an impromptu break on moving day to look through old photo albums or yearbooks—a complete momentum wrecker. Again, trust that proper LAMP technique will return you to these interesting postings within two hours, supported by both a solid strategy and peace of mind.

Now add your third check mark.

LIST	ADVOCACY	MOTIVATION	POSTING
✓			
✓			
✓			

APPROACH #4: TRENDING EMPLOYERS

By now, your list should have around thirty possible employers—ten (or more!) from each of the three previous approaches. This final ten-minute brainstorming approach consists of reading the news. Online or print is fine—just whatever you read organically. Are you a regular reader of *Fast Company*, or do you prefer the health headlines in the *Huffington Post*, or *PC Gamer* or *Forbes*? Either way, read for fun for ten minutes, but anytime you come across an organization doing something interesting in these areas you enjoy learning about, add it to your L column if it's not already there.

Again, we spend so much time in our day-to-day lives learning about topics of genuine interest for free—I just want to find a way for you to get paid for doing so.

Cognitive Drift

In any database, but especially in Indeed.com, be sure to maximize the number of results shown on any one screen (and choose "Show all" whenever possible). The default view on Indeed.com is ten hits per page, but you can increase that to fifty, reducing by up to 80 percent the number of clicks you need to make to see all relevant results. Why does this matter?

SuperFreakonomics authors Steven Levitt and Stephen Dubner highlight a study that says cognitive drift sets in anytime a computer user must wait more than a second after a mouse is clicked for the screen to change. So each click represents an opportunity for distraction if a website is slow to load.

Thus, change this setting in all of your job posting websites, alumni databases, shopping portals, and so on.

Shouldn't I stay close to what I already know rather than what I'm interested in learning about?

Theoretically, yes, but while your existing knowledge may help you get an initial conversation, your lack of genuine interest in that topic will make networking both excruciating and unsustainable. Furthermore, one of employers' biggest red flags in a candidate is disengagement, so trying to get a potential advocate to incur personal risk in order to get you an interview is prohibitively difficult if you aren't interested in what your contacts have to teach you—regardless of your current experience or level of seniority.

What if I don't have any existing interests I learn about on a regular basis?

If you don't have any interests you are naturally learning about, pick an industry or function you think you *may* enjoy reading about for ten minutes—for instance, machine learning or food science—and

Google it along with the word *trends*. A number of articles will appear, and given the simplicity of your search terms, they are likely to be macro level, which is perfect for someone trying to learn more about a new industry.

Another alternative: Google a list of venture capital firms (like Sequoia Capital and Accel) and see which employers *they're* excited enough about to invest in and why. These usually cover a wide array of industries, so something is bound to strike your fancy and give you something to work with.

One last suggestion: Look up start-ups that have headquarters based in your current city (and neighboring towns) on Crunchbase, and read up on how those employers' respective categories are defined

Time Out #4

"Intern" Beware

The process for an internship search is identical to that for a full-time job search, with one modification—internship seekers should be careful about using the word *intern* when using job search engines. Far fewer internships than full-time positions are posted online, and adding the word *intern* to your search terms in job search engines will dramatically reduce the quantity of your results—typically by a factor of one hundred.

That does not mean the word should be avoided—use it early and often! If you find too few results are being returned for internships, "intern" is the first word you should remove from your search terms. Even if an organization is not posting internships right now (in fact, some organizations that regularly take on interns never post internships at all), the fact that they're recruiting full-time employees suggests a future need for interns.

You will make one more slight change to the process when we get to the Posting column in chapter 4, but other than that, 2HJS works exactly the same for you as for someone seeking full-time employment!

on the site, which you can learn by clicking the employer's name. (Note that Crunchbase will only show you the first five results of your search for free, but you can keep adding criteria to locate a slightly different top five.) This will give you a better idea of which small and medium-sized businesses (SMBs) are available to you locally.

Keep in mind that the less readily apparent the employer is, the less competition there is likely to be and the further a single unit of networking effort with them will carry you, since smaller employers are not accustomed to receiving proactive interest—especially interest that doesn't originate from a job posting.

This method not only informs but also identifies smaller organizations that are looking to get their name out. Attracting qualified talent may be an expensive proposition for these organizations, so job seekers who approach *them*, driven by a genuine interest in their line of business, will enjoy a significant advantage.

Job seekers I've worked with who approach employers found through this method have in some cases advanced immediately to a final-round interview, simply because they showed initiative in finding that employer in the first place. Regardless, the "trending employer" brainstorming approach gives you critical information about which sectors are hiring, where and how the market is changing, and which organizations are best positioned to take advantage of those market shifts.

Now you're ready to highlight the L column in your spreadsheet and sort it alphabetically to screen out duplicate entries. And that's the end of the L task! Forty minutes and forty or more employers later, your LAMP list should look something like this (an example that we further develop and reference for the remainder of the book).

#	LIST	ADVOCACY	MOTIVATION	POSTING
1	Ace Tomato Co.			
2	BiffCo			
3	Darlington Electronics			
4	Hanso Corporation			
5	Initech			
...	...			
...	...			
...	...			
39	Staypuft Marshmallow Inc.			
40	Zamunda Airlines			

By eating the job search elephant one ten-minute bite at a time, you have completed a list of forty employers in forty minutes. Well done!

LIST	ADVOCACY	MOTIVATION	POSTING
✓			
✓			
✓			
✓			

And with that fourth check mark, we can bid the entire L step adieu.

LIST	ADVOCACY	MOTIVATION	POSTING
✓			

TROUBLESHOOTING

What if I am an international citizen seeking to work in the United States, but I lack permanent US work authorization, which some of my target employers require?

The process is still essentially the same, but because you will need your future employer to sponsor a US work visa (usually an H-1B visa), you should populate your LAMP list as much as possible with organizations found in the US Department of Labor's annual list of employers who sponsored such visas last year. Our best assumption is that employers who sponsored relevant visas last year are more likely to sponsor visas again this year than those who did not.

A number of online vendors offer free and paid versions of this same list, but I personally use Myvisajobs.com (free as of this writing), since it provides the ability to sort the government's H-1B report *by career*. When a desired career is selected, it will tell you which employers sponsored the most H-1B visas for those careers, listing them in descending order from most to least visas sponsored.

In your case, I recommend replacing the ten-minute "trending employers" approach with employers you find in your H-1B searches. In fact, if you want to populate your list entirely with employers you find using this method, I would support that as well. Just be sure to familiarize yourself with all the other brainstorming methods since each offers its own unique value for helping you define a coherent set of target employers. Also remember not to rule out SMBs simply because they're smaller and you've never heard of them.

SMBs are less likely to have formal rules about the work authorization requirements of potential hires—they may simply want to hire the best candidate possible, regardless of the individual's background. Remember, hiring managers are more interested in finding good enough talent quickly than perfect talent slowly, so if you are an otherwise superior talent to what they would find in a US-only talent pool, and you find them instead of vice versa, you may be surprised how willing they are to work with you.

Regardless, it is incumbent on you to educate yourself on your visa requirements and/or consult an immigration attorney to learn how to best explain your sponsorship situation to potential employers. Many immigration attorneys provide such advice for free in the hope you'll later choose their firm to actually do your paperwork filing for you, so don't be shy about asking!

## CHAPTER 2

ADVOCACY

 **10 MINUTES**

Why is advocacy so important?
Isn't 2HJS about using technology?

It *is* counterintuitive—one might assume technology would make connections, contacts, and other human advocacy unnecessary in the modern job search, but in fact that support is more important now than ever before.

In both college and graduate school, I had always heard that alumni are a critical part of the job search, but for most of my life, I never really understood why. When I was an undergrad in the late nineties, the economy was dot-com strong. It felt like there were enough jobs for everyone. Alumni to me were just nice old people who'd show up on campus to describe their employers.

Fast-forward to my years at business school in the early 2000s. The dot-com bubble had burst, and the economy had slowed dramatically. Jobs were still available through campus recruiting, but there was much more competition for each one and it was the visiting alumni deciding who got them. Those "nice old people" suddenly had a material impact on my ability to find employment!

I went from totally disregarding alumni to obsessing over them. However, while I had heard countless times that I should "network" in the job search, I had never learned how to actually do so. Complicating matters, I was awkward, so my attempts to strike up a conversation were perhaps even more uncomfortable for alumni as they were for me.

At the time, this shift felt incredibly unfair. Being qualified on paper used to be sufficient (or at least a great advantage) in the job search—now it was inadequate by itself.

Qualified candidates to this day—on university campuses and beyond—still require *internal advocacy* to raise their credentials above the noise of the hundreds of casually submitted resumes that online job postings have enabled. 2HJS was developed to create this critical network of internal advocates quickly and efficiently.

Before we fill in our A column, though, I have some good news— you have completed the hardest part of this process! 2HJS from here on is like a highly effective autopilot—it takes over during the tedious but necessary job search steps so you can conserve your time and energy for the steps that are more sophisticated and engaging, like gaining the trust of those potential advocates you'll have identified once we complete our LAMP list.

If filling in your L column felt like an art, the remainder of your LAMP list will feel more like science. Furthermore, if you followed the guidance from Time Out #2 on page 42, you'll be done in even less time than the ten minutes we've allotted to this step. So get ready to make a lot of progress quickly.

So why an A column?

The columns of your LAMP list are not perfect information. Perfect information for this column would be, "Will someone at this employer help me get an interview?" But because that would be difficult to obtain in advance, we need to find a *proxy* (another word for *substitute*) for that perfect information. The best proxy for the *likelihood of finding a sympathetic contact* at a target employer is finding out if

Making West Virginia Eat Healthier

Chip and Dan Heath, in their excellent book *Switch*, confront how to create change when change is hard. One critical element of invoking change, they describe is "scripting the critical moves" (providing specific, actionable instructions for accomplishing a goal). They tell the story of two health researchers in West Virginia who identified a dire need for state residents to adopt a healthier diet. Instructing West Virginians in eating healthier was unlikely to produce any real results. They had to think of a more specific way to create a change in diet.

The researchers adopted the 80/20 Rule. They saw that whole milk was very popular, especially in rural communities. However, it's also the single largest source of saturated fat (the bad kind) in the average American's diet. So they focused there since a majority of Americans drink milk.

Piloting their concept in two communities, they ran radio and TV ads encouraging residents not vaguely (to "eat healthier") but specifically (to buy 1 percent milk instead of whole milk), illustrating the point in their ads by equating the amount of saturated fat in a glass of whole milk to five strips of bacon or bringing a tube full of the same amount of saturated fat as in a gallon of whole milk to press conferences. They also cleverly noted that families drink whatever's in the refrigerator, so they saw that the key was to change the purchasing behavior of West Virginians—their consumption behavior would naturally follow.

This specific approach was effective. In the pilot communities, the market share of low-fat milk shot up from 18 percent before the campaign to 41 percent immediately after, and it held at 35 percent six months later. By providing clear direction, a difficult change was achieved.

Consider 2HJS to be the path for fundamentally changing the way you approach the job search. While you are following this book's explicit instructions for executing an effective search, millions of other job seekers will be struggling to put advice like "use your network" to practical use (the job search equivalent of being told to eat healthier), giving you a significant advantage.

Remember, you are the bachelor in this process! Winning is inevitable—it just takes the right infrastructure (this book) and a little bit of time.

someone like you currently works there, whether it's an alum of your most recent university, a fellow military veteran, or a close friend or family member. *That* we can do quickly.

So how exactly do I look up advocates for forty employers in ten minutes?

The answer is simple: focus. We are going to shut our brains off and become job searching assembly lines for the next forty minutes.

By simplifying a complex process to a series of individual tasks repeated over and over, we will increase our efficiency and reduce the mental effort required. Focusing on a repetitive task may be boring, but it's a nice break from thinking all day, every day. Plus, it helps get things done quickly and effectively.

How do I complete my A column if I have access to alumni from a previous educational institution or program?

If you have access to alumni from a previous school or program you attended, bring up the custom search screen in LinkedIn (see Technology Corner #2 on page 39 for a refresher).

Put your most recent educational program into the Schools field. Note that, as of this printing, there are two places you can enter school information—you want to use the one that autocompletes, making it easier for you to find the specific program from which you graduated. This is especially important if your most recent program was a graduate school of a larger university—you want to look for alumni of your graduate program rather than the larger university, since the latter are less likely to be relevant for your future networking purposes.

Next, starting with the first employer in your L column, enter that employer's name into the Current Companies field (again, you want the one that autocompletes rather than the one that does not—this helps ensure you are looking up the right organization) and hit Enter.

If one or more alumni *of your most recent program* are currently employed at that employer, enter Y for "yes." Otherwise, enter N for "no" and repeat the process for the second employer in your L column. Lather, rinse, and repeat.

Did you remember to highlight the employers (Time Out #2, page 42) you found using the alumni/affinity brainstorming method? If so, that's great news! You just saved some time! Simply give all those highlighted employers a Y, since we know by the way we found them that at least one of our cohort currently works for them.

The temptation here is to copy the alumni information you find or even worse, to copy *and format* that information. (Counting the alumni is also unnecessary.) This is wasted effort. Recall that for most of these employers, you will never need more alumni information than the Y or N, and for those you do, you may need it for just one person.

How do I complete my A column if I *don't* have access to alumni from a previous educational institution?

Don't fret. It just means you'll get your LAMP list done even faster! What we are trying to do with this Advocacy column is approximate the likelihood of finding a sympathetic contact. There are a number of different ways to do this without an alumni database, but the three best approaches are (1) friends and family, (2) proximity to your current residence, and (3) similarity to your previous experience.

For option 1, simply start at the top of your L column and for each employer name you read, enter a Y if you can immediately think of a friend or family member that works there who may advocate for you. That's it. Don't overthink this! Friends and family are often very helpful sources of advocacy when trying to gain employment (even for those who have alumni connections), so use the 80/20 Rule here and finish your L column a bit early!

For option 2, start at the top of your L column and enter Y in the A column if the employer is within current commuting distance and

N if otherwise. Some employers (at least initially) only consider local candidates when attempting to fill a position to avoid having to cover the cost of relocating a new employee (or risk that new employee deciding not to relocate). Thus it will be easier for you to get advocacy from employees at local employers than from those a move away.

For option 3, for each employer in your L column, estimate whether your previous experience makes you immediately credible with employees at that organization. If, for example, you have relevant industry experience (e.g., you are approaching an automaker, and you had worked for one of their suppliers in the past), enter Y in the A column. Otherwise, enter N and move to the next employer on your list.

An N in the A column does not disqualify you from approaching these employers! In fact, it shows initiative when you reach out to them despite having no easy "in." By the end of your 2HJS experience, again, you will be completely unfazed about whether you have any current contacts at an organization—you'll be so accustomed to making them "on demand" that you'll be able to relax and just focus on what targets appeal to you most.

With that introduction, start populating your column! You'll be done before you know it, leaving you with something that looks like this:

#	LIST	ADVOCACY	MOTIVATION	POSTING
1	Ace Tomato Co.	Y		
2	BiffCo	Y		
3	Darlington Electronics	N		
4	Hanso Corporation	Y		
5	Initech	N		
...	...	...		
...	...	...		
...	...	...		
39	Staypuft Marshmallow Inc.	N		
40	Zamunda Airlines	Y		

And with that . . .

LIST	ADVOCACY	MOTIVATION	POSTING
✓	✓		

We can now move on to the third part of our LAMP list—we're halfway there!

TROUBLESHOOTING

What if my school(s) have relatively few alumni?

There is no minimum number of alumni you need to have for your list—some lists I've seen have had under 5 percent of their A column populated by Ys. That just makes the smaller number all the more important to identify up front! Furthermore, even if we have all Ns in our A column, it simply means we won't use Advocacy to sort our employers at the end of our LAMP list. For right now, we just want to get a sense of how big and relevant our existing network is.

What if I have been out of school for many years?

You may consider substituting in your immediate (also known as first-degree) LinkedIn connections in lieu of literal alumni connections for your A column if you think it is more relevant and/or you have a large existing LinkedIn network.

However, recognize that the longer you have been on LinkedIn, the more out-of-date many of your connections have become. If you find you are unfamiliar with most of the connections who appear, default to your most recent academic program or substitute an affinity group that better captures your current network. The same goes for second-degree connections, especially if its been a long time since you last interacted with your shared connection. At that point, second-degree connection is a second-degree stranger. We'll talk more about this in chapter 5.

TROUBLESHOOTING

Does the same go for Instagram/Facebook/Twitter? Should I start building my network there as well?

You could, but they won't be as directly applicable to your job search as LinkedIn, given their social rather than professional focus. That said, follow the lead of your target industries. If you're in the visual arts, Instagram will likely be a must. If you're targeting journalism, Twitter will similarly be critical.

I used my graduate school's alumni population to complete my Advocacy list. Should I now check my undergraduate school's alumni database?

No! If you have a graduate degree, there is no need to search your undergraduate school's database right now. Similarly, if you used your school's alumni population on LinkedIn to populate your A column, there is no need to repeat the process using your school's alumni database. We'll go back and dig deeper for connections on an as needed basis but only as needed at the end of our LAMP process.

CHAPTER 3

MOTIVATION

 5 MINUTES

I already know Motivation is important, so can I skip this chapter?

Definitely not. It's both the most important and the most overlooked step of the process—a devastating combination. Plus, it literally takes only five minutes. This section will take you longer to read than it will to execute, but doing both will save you a lot of time down the road, because this will be the most important criterion we sort our list by once it is completed.

What is so important about Motivation?

Motivation is the engine that ultimately drives your job search forward. Thus it is *the single most important* factor when ranking your targets. Even if I give you perfect instructions for conducting a job search, without your willingness to execute those instructions, success is impossible. Plus, every time you send an email requesting an informational meeting (which we cover in Part 2: Contact), you're more likely to get ignored than you are to get a response! Therefore, your Motivation score is effectively a proxy for your *pain tolerance* for approaching that particular employer, because it's easier to dig deep and contact a fourth person (after the first three ignore you) at a dream employer than at a backup.

So I *shouldn't* pursue backup employers?

Absolutely, you should—in fact, 2HJS requires you to! Just don't *start* with them. That's why we make a LAMP list—to ensure you don't do precisely that.

Too often I see people begin their job searches by spending valuable time pursuing employers in whom they are not very interested. However, this is backward. In practice, your interest level (or Motivation, in LAMP parlance) is a *far* better predictor of success than either the existence of relevant job postings or relevant experience in a no-longer-interesting field.

Less successful job seekers tend to adopt this backups-first approach for one of three main reasons: (1) the application is convenient or easy, (2) they think their relevant experience will improve their chances, hoping (futilely) interviewers won't detect their lack of desire, or (3) they see a posting and get momentarily inspired to "make progress." Certainly, it's important to strike when the motivation iron is hot. However, following inspiration and pursuing backup employers before ideal ones randomly throws job seekers grievously off course, with *sunk costs* rather than genuine interest driving future efforts.

What are sunk costs, and what do they have to do with the job search?

Sunk costs are expenses (not just of money, but also of time and effort) that cannot be recovered. Let's say I buy a ticket to go see the latest *Transformers* movie, and I realize about thirty minutes in that it's terrible. Offensively bad. Even so, I may be tempted to watch the remaining two hours because I paid good money to watch this trainwreck.

However, the ticket price is a sunk cost—I can't get that money back. I'm out fifteen dollars whether I stay or go. Similarly, since I can't ever get back the time I've already invested in this travesty, it is also a sunk cost.

But walking away is *hard*. This is the risk of sunk costs—you start making decisions based on previous decisions you regret rather than on rational criteria. According to economics, the rational action is to disregard sunk costs—my fifteen-dollar ticket and time already invested—and go do something else of higher entertainment value. Watching traffic lights change, for example.

Without a completed LAMP list in your job search, sunk costs can lead you to start unintentionally prioritizing poor targets at the expense of richer ones. For example, let's say you see a posting for Employer X, whom you find underwhelming as a potential employer, but you become momentarily inspired to "make it happen" and apply anyway. At this point, your future decision making is susceptible to corruption by sunk costs.

As you continue reviewing postings in the future, your rational brain now thinks, "If I applied to Employer X, then I should also apply to every employer I like *more* than Employer X." Depending on how little you liked Employer X, this can result in an impossibly large to-do list.

In Vegas they call this "throwing good money after bad" or investing more money into an already bad bet. The right approach—both in Vegas and in the job search—is to walk away from bad investments. However, this is much easier said than done.

Walking away requires nerve, and nerves fray quickly in the job search. Once we randomly apply to a proverbial Employer X, the internal debate about whether to embrace or shun that shotgun approach can itself wear a job seeker out, resulting in the true worst-case scenario: exhaustion without anything to show for it.

So how do I avoid becoming a victim of sunk costs?

Don't do anything *randomly* in the job search. There is nothing random in this book—we've already decided which employers are in our initial consideration set (otherwise known as everything in our L column), and we will let the data from our LAMP list dictate the order in which we pursue them.

In this Motivation step, we leverage a concept called *arbitrary coherence* to quickly yet accurately categorize our level of interest in each potential target. This step couldn't be simpler. It takes only five minutes and requires no research (it *forbids* it, in fact!), but it is perhaps the most ignored step of the job search, even though it saves job seekers dozens of hours of headaches, confusion, and anxiety.

What is arbitrary coherence? Why does it enable this step to go so quickly?

In his classic text *Psychometric Theory*, the late Vanderbilt professor Jum Nunnally wrote:

> Whereas people are notoriously inaccurate in judging the absolute magnitudes of stimuli, e.g., the length of a line in inches, they are notoriously accurate in making comparative judgments.

In short, we measure poorly, but we compare well. For example, imagine I show you a brand-new lawnmower and I ask you to rate its appeal on a scale from 1 to 10, with 10 being highest.

Most of you won't have previous experience rating lawnmowers, so your answer will be meaningless to me without further explanation. Basically, if you score it a 5, I won't know what 5 means. You may have been playing it safe with the scale provided because you have no idea whether you'll like future lawnmowers better or worse. Conversely, you may have *hated* the lawnmower but would never rate anything you couldn't make yourself lower than a 5. I simply don't know.

Once I ask you to rate a second and third lawnmower, however, your ratings start to make sense relative to one another. I still don't know what a 5 means, but I know with a high degree of certainty that you like a 5 a little bit less than a 6 and much less than a 9 or 10.

Arbitrary coherence is a concept that says that, although an initial rating of 1 in a series of items is largely arbitrary (and can be highly influenced by random suggestions), subsequent ratings will be coherent with respect to the first one.[1] In other words, the relative ratings will be correct, even if the absolute values are useless.

Most novice job seekers tend to begin with a too-small universe of possible target employers. When I see a target list with only a handful of employers on it, I have no idea whether those employers are truly that job seeker's favorite targets or simply the first employers that came to mind or showed up in a search for job postings. I'm regularly shocked by how little thought job seekers give to identifying potential targets; convenience is the most common driving force, so when pursuing the employer ceases to be convenient (which it always does), many job seekers lose their desire to continue pursuit.

In this book, we employ some job search jujitsu to use arbitrary coherence—our susceptibility to largely arbitrary initial opinions—to our advantage. We declare an arbitrary anchor—in this case, we classify our favorite target employer as a 3—and rate all our employers relative to that one on a scale of 0 to 3.

How does this step actually work, then?

In this step, we vertically work our way down the Motivation column, filling in Motivation scores one by one for each of our targets.

Starting with the first employer in your LAMP list, rate your level of interest in pursuing each one on a scale of 0 to 3, *using only the information you know about each employer right now.* Your score should be a blended average of how interesting you find everything you know about this employer at the present moment—their brand name, sector, location, size, growth, proximity, and so on—all in one simple number. However, no outside research or consideration of current job postings and/or your own qualifications are allowed at this time (I'll explain why in a moment).

Remember, your favorite employers are 3s, so middle-tier choices are 2s and lower-tier choices are 1s. Reserve 0s for target employers we don't know enough about right now to have an informed opinion. We'll selectively research some of these 0s *after* our LAMP list is completed, but under no circumstances should you research these targets right now—not even to find out what they do or where they're located—because, as described in chapter 1, to maintain efficiency we must avoid switching between dissimilar tasks.

Researching facts is the polar opposite of providing general opinions, so the risk here of losing your place is higher than you might think. So don't think; just read each employer's name and react. In five minutes you'll have a beautiful, completely filled-in M column that looks something like this:

#	LIST	ADVOCACY	MOTIVATION	POSTING
1	Ace Tomato Co.	Y	2	
2	BiffCo	Y	3	
3	Darlington Electronics	N	2	
4	Hanso Corporation	Y	1	
5	Initech	N	0	
...	...	...	...	
...	...	...	...	
...	...	...	...	
39	Staypuft Marshmallow Inc.	N	3	
40	Zamunda Airlines	Y	0	

In my book, that earns you another check mark:

LIST	ADVOCACY	MOTIVATION	POSTING
✓	✓	✓	

We're just a fifteen-minute step away from finishing the fourth and final column of our LAMP list, the Posting column, and learning which employers are worth our time and which need to go find themselves a different Bachelor!

TROUBLESHOOTING

What if relocating to (or remaining in) a certain area is essential to my search, but I don't know where many of my LAMP list employers are located?

In those cases, temporarily disregard location in your Motivation rating for that employer. Award it your preferred rating minus 0.5 points, leaving you with a score of 2.5 for a dream employer, for example. (Make sure your spreadsheet is set to show you one decimal place, in this case—you don't want to see your 2.5 automatically turn into a 3 because of formatting.)

Once we sort our list, we'll see whether any employers with Motivation scores ending in 0.5 are close to the top of our list, and we can change our Motivation score up or down according to location.

What if I don't have any or many 1s (or any other number) in my M column? Is that okay?

This is totally fine. Most of my students don't use many 1s either, because most employers they knew well enough to give 1s to were screened out before they were included in the L column. The 1 rating—if used at all—tends to show up most often when a list of employers meeting certain criteria during the L step was copied and pasted into the L column wholesale.

TROUBLESHOOTING

What if a majority of my ratings are 0s because I'm not familiar with the employers in this industry/region?

That is just fine, and a great illustration of how LAMP saves you time. Before LAMP, you might have felt obligated to research all those employers individually, which likely would require hours of effort. Using LAMP, we leave them all as 0s for now, and once our list is complete, we'll see whether any of those 0s give us a reason to believe they warrant further research.

## CHAPTER 4

POSTING

15 MINUTES

Didn't we already use job postings in the L column of our LAMP list?

Yes, we did, but in this final chapter of Part 1: Prioritize, we're going to use a job search engine to fill in an entirely separate Posting column. In this column we will rate the *relevance* of job postings an employer currently has available. Those with more relevant postings are more time-sensitive (and therefore higher-priority) targets; thus they will get a higher score in your P column, just as you gave higher Motivation scores to the employers you found more interesting in our last step.

But didn't you compare job postings to "black holes" earlier?

Yes, I did. I know it's a bit contradictory—that something could both be helpful and a waste of time—but let me explain. Online job postings (and the job search engines that find them for you) are helpful in several ways, but they are *terrible* at actually getting you a job. Their real value is the meta-information they provide.

What is meta-information?

The Oxford English Dictionary defines the prefix *meta-* as "self-referential," so meta-information is information about information itself.

I have two good friends, Hank and Katie. Hank is a true savant—he knows everything. He remembers everything he reads, and he reads *a lot.* He's therefore a mainstay on my weekly trivia team. Katie, on the other hand, doesn't know everything in the same way Hank does, but she can find information extraordinarily well. Need a current article about the cotton candy market in Canada? No problem. Want a scholarly paper identifying the best aromatherapy scents for curing a toothache? She's on it.

In other words, Hank has a gift for *information*, whereas Katie has a gift for *meta*-information. The good news for Katie is that meta-information is a greater asset in today's job search than information itself.

Before online job postings flourished, finding out which employers were hiring was the main challenge. Now it's easy to find out who's hiring—it's just impossible to get their attention. Knowing the identity of the hiring manager is helpful information, but it is a one-off luxury rather than a strategy. Knowing how to systematically *find* the hiring manager is meta-information, and it's crucial in the modern job search.

So, if online job postings aren't good for getting you a job, how do they work for the P step?

Job postings—more specifically, job search engines like Indeed.com—provide great information about what sorts of jobs are available in a particular city, as you learned during the L step in chapter 1. However, for the P step, we're more interested in a job search engine's ability to tell us who's actively hiring right now versus who is not.

The data we've collected in each of these last three steps—Advocacy (chapter 2), Motivation (chapter 3), and now Posting—is itself meta-information. It's a proxy for more important information—facts that would be prohibitively difficult or time-consuming to determine precisely. So we're using a quick 80/20 Rule approach instead.

What are the A, M, and P columns proxy information for again?

Your Advocacy column is a proxy for the likelihood of finding a sympathetic contact at that employer and for the employer's willingness to value someone with your background and skill set. Your Motivation column is a proxy for your interest level and thus your willingness to actually do the work necessary to get that job. Remember, while connections can get you a foothold, authenticity and follow-through are what get you the job.

This Posting column is a proxy for urgency. We know that as soon as employers post a job, they become overwhelmed by applicants, so if one of your top targets has posted a job, you must find an advocate there ASAP. Postponing your outreach to those firms for a week or two may take you out of the running.

How do I fill in the P column, then?

The P column takes about fifteen minutes for a forty-employer list—longer lists will take more time, but only marginally so. However, the temptation to cheat here will be significant—you will return to Indeed.com (featured earlier in our L step) to search for postings, but you *must not* click on any interesting ones you find—use only the search results themselves (that is, job titles, locations, and brief descriptions) to make your decisions! Trust me: if you do this step correctly, you'll be back to those perfect job postings within thirty minutes, but if you do it incorrectly, it will take hours and you may get sidetracked entirely, rendering all efforts to get to this point meaningless. Rest assured, we are very close to done.

I have tested several different job search engines head-to-head, and as of this book's printing, Indeed.com has consistently been the most comprehensive. It also operates the same way in over fifty countries. The website's interface consists only of entry fields for "what" and "where." In this step we're only concerned with "what." However, unlike the way we used Indeed.com in the L step—starting with keywords, job titles, and locations—this time we're going to start with the employer names from our LAMP list to see what hiring they are doing right now.

This will be an 80/20 search, though—we're looking for good enough information quickly, rather than perfect information slowly. Done right, this step takes only fifteen minutes, but that involves adopting a policy of strategic ignorance—in other words, you need to willingly ignore *interesting* information because it is not *critical* information.

Let your competition waste their time clicking through these tedious and long-winded postings. (Spoiler alert: Employers will always ask for more experience than you have, so spare yourself the needless anxiety.) You'll simply classify the urgency and relevance of an employer's hiring activity based on just the search results themselves, the job title, the location, and the short description provided. Then we move to the next employer on our list. Just as in the Advocacy step, the details aren't important right now—we can go back for those later. The high-level information is what we're after—in this case, "Are they hiring people like me for positions I'm interested in?"

Again, we start with the employer at the top of the list and systematically work our way down, rating each employer as we go.

Finding very relevant job postings for each target employer is the best-case scenario. However, sometimes you'll find less relevant job postings, such as positions in a different department or at a higher level. This gives you the important meta-information that *somewhat* relevant hiring is under way—meaning HR is actively engaging in talent identification for people *like* (if not exactly) you.

That's a better signal of potential employment than no remotely relevant postings at all.

To get this step done quickly, we need to be systematic. Thus we search each employer for an ideal posting—if we find one, the employer gets a score of 3. If we don't, we search again for any semi-relevant postings. If we find any, the employer gets a score of 2; if not, it gets a 1. Then we move to the next employer, and so on.

To search for an ideal posting, we first enter the employer's name into the Indeed.com "What" field, followed by a probable keyword or keywords about the job we're seeking. For example, let's assume you're an aspiring graphic designer. The first employer in the sample LAMP list is "Ace Tomato Co.," so our "What" field should look like this when we press Enter:

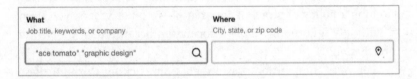

Technology Corner #3

Use of Quotes in Search Fields

Place keywords that contain two or more words in quotation marks to indicate you are seeking an exact match. If you don't—for example, if you search for "operations engineer" without quotes instead of with them—any relevant search results will be overwhelmed by many unrelated ones featuring "operations" and "engineer" separately in different contexts.

If Indeed.com finds any matching job postings, it will list the job title, the posting's website address, and a couple lines of text from the posting that include your keywords—something like this:

This information alone is sufficient for us to determine Ace Tomato's Posting score. This is an essential point, so allow me to say it once more, with feeling: DO NOT CLICK THROUGH ON THESE JOB POSTINGS! Doing so will obliterate your time, efficiency, and energy—guaranteed.

Job seekers' overwhelming temptation upon finding an ideal posting is to drop everything and race to complete the online application. Remember, though, that submitting a resume online is meaningless without an internal advocate and a lot of follow-up effort. (There is truly no benefit to being first, let alone three hundredth, in a pile of resumes nobody will ever look at!)

Therefore, it is better to hold off on initiating contact with your targets until you know which ones are top priorities. This course of action may even make the online application entirely unnecessary—if, for example, you find the right contact or decide the target is not a priority—saving you even more time. All that matters for us right now is, "Is this employer's Posting score a 3, 2, or 1?"

Back to our example—if we get zero results from our "'Ace Tomato' 'graphic design'" search, we do not give Ace Tomato a Posting score of 3, but we do not yet know if it warrants a score of 2 or 1. To see if it gets a Posting score of 2, we repeat the search without the functional keyword and just the company name:

If we get back any postings here—particularly in semi-related departments, like marketing communications or multimedia support—we should give Ace Tomato a Posting score of 2 for "somewhat relevant hiring activity." However, if the results are for roles that aren't even tangentially connected to what we want to do, or we get no results at all, we can safely assume there are no relevant openings and give it a Posting score of 1.

Granted, Ace Tomato may actually have relevant openings—job search engines aren't perfect, and not all jobs get posted online. However, the important fact is that their openings are not *easy to find*—for us or anyone else—so you don't have to worry about a flood of competition swooping in to claim that hidden opportunity before you can.

After entering our Posting score for Ace Tomato, we replace "Ace Tomato" with our next employer's name, BiffCo, resulting in a "What" field in Indeed.com that looks like this:

And we repeat the process until we've completely filled in our LAMP list Posting column for all targets, using this general guidance:

POSTING COLUMN SCORE	IF SEEKING A *FULL-TIME JOB* AND YOU FIND MATCHES FOR:
3	Employer & functional keyword *"Ace Tomato" "graphic design"*
2	Employer only *"Ace Tomato"*
1	n/a *No matches found for above*

This step moves fast if we stay focused; we can complete a forty-employer LAMP list in about fifteen minutes. We'll discuss how to sort our completed LAMP list shortly.

Are there alternatives to a 3-point rating scale for postings? If so, when should I use them?

Some users choose to make this a simple Yes/No column (like we did for the Advocacy column). One reason a job seeker may do this is because the job they are seeking has no consistent title—for example, what one employer calls a "consultant" another might call an "associate," so the job seeker just searches the employer on Indeed.com without any functional keywords and judges the employer's relevance from that search alone. If you find you're not getting a lot of value from the 3-point scale, feel free to switch it to a Yes/No.

When is using a 3-point scale especially important?

There are two circumstances when a 3-point scale is a must: when you are seeking an internship (this is the slight change for internship seekers I referenced back in chapter 1) or when you have a specialized degree or relevant credential.

For internship seekers, a 3-point scale is critical for two reasons: first, internship opportunities are posted online far less frequently than full-time jobs (meaning most of your entries would be "No" if you relied on a Yes/No format); and second, relevant full-time jobs (meaning full-time versions of what you're seeking as an internship) are predictive of internship needs, either because an employer has difficulty finding a full-time hire and needs a stopgap employee such as an intern or because the employer wishes to establish a pipeline of talent for future full-time hiring needs.

In other words, when seeking an internship, consider relevant, full-time roles to be "somewhat relevant" (for a score of 2), as in the table on the following page:

POSTING COLUMN SCORE	IF SEEKING AN INTERNSHIP AND YOU FIND MATCHES FOR:
3	Employer, functional keyword & "intern" *"Ace Tomato" "graphic design" intern*
2	Employer & functional keyword *"Ace Tomato" "graphic design"*
1	n/a *No matches found for above*

If you have a specialty degree (like an RN, JD, or MBA) or a relevant credential (like the ability to code in C++), that degree or credential should be a part of all of your job posting searches, as in the following table:

POSTING COLUMN SCORE	IF SEEKING A JOB WITH A SPECIALTY DEGREE/RELEVANT CREDENTIAL AND YOU FIND MATCHES FOR:
3	Employer, specialty degree/relevant credential & functional keyword *"Ace Tomato" mba marketing; "Ace Tomato" C++ developer*
2	Employer & specialty degree/relevant credential *"Ace Tomato" mba; "Ace Tomato" C++*
1	n/a *No matches found for above*

Should I sign up for Indeed.com alerts?

Requesting job search alerts is a very efficient way to conduct a reactive search—one in which you wait for postings to go live and then reach out to the employers in question (or apply directly). However,

I don't advocate this approach, precisely *because* it is reactive—at least until you've started your first round of outreach to your Top 5.

Postings are nice information to have, but Motivation is ultimately the most important driver of this process, as you'll see shortly. Getting Posting information once, up front, as a "snapshot in time" is ideal, because this process is designed to help you execute a *proactive* plan for your top-choice employers *right now*.

Constantly rechecking for new postings takes you away from proactive strategy back to a reactive, shotgun approach to the job search. However, if you are curious, set yourself a reminder to look further into setting up job search alerts *after* you complete Part 2 of this book (chapters 5 to 7). Once that's complete, you will have some natural downtime while waiting for your contacts to respond to you, so that's a good time to learn how to sign up for new posting alerts, if desired.

Once I complete my list, how do I sort it?

If all goes well, our (unsorted) list should finally end up looking something like this:

#	LIST	ADVOCACY	MOTIVATION	POSTING
1	Ace Tomato Co.	Y	2	1
2	BiffCo	Y	3	3
3	Darlington Electronics	N	2	2
4	Hanso Corporation	Y	1	3
5	Initech	N	0	3
...	...	...	...	...
...	...	...	...	...
39	Staypuft Marshmallow Inc.	N	3	3
40	Zamunda Airlines	Y	0	1

With that, our Posting column is complete! All that remains is to sort the list and ensure that it is ordered properly. We'll cover this in a brief Part 1: Prioritize Wrap-Up section at the end of this chapter—but for now, congratulations are in order. You've compiled all the raw data necessary to complete your very first LAMP list!

LIST	ADVOCACY	MOTIVATION	POSTING
✓	✓	✓	✓

TROUBLESHOOTING

My target employers (for example, venture capital firms) tend not to post jobs online. Can I skip this step?

If you found that Indeed.com did not help you find any relevant postings during the L step of this process, you may skip this step and fill in all your selections as 1s. This essentially cancels it as a prioritization factor, so you'll be relying only on Motivation and Advocacy, but the process is still fundamentally the same, even if your entire Posting column is all 1s.

However, sometimes there are ways other than current job postings to approximate urgency. For example, tech start-ups who have just received a new round of funding would be much more time-sensitive targets for finding an advocate than start-ups who haven't gotten a new round of funding in a while. Thus you may choose to use a freely available funding database like Crunchbase, AngelList, or even LinkedIn's company pages (which list funding amount, date, and round in their About sections) to identify how recently a target employer has received new funding.

In this case, you may choose to award a Posting score of 3 (out of 3) to a start-up who's gotten new funding in the last three months—remember that the Posting column approximates urgency, and few things advertise an urgent need to develop an internal advocate than a big infusion of cash!

TROUBLESHOOTING

You may then choose to award a Posting score of 2 to start-ups who haven't received new funding within the last three months but have received new funding in the last year—they may have accounted for all that new funding already but may still have some cash available. Finally, you may choose to award a score of 1 to start-ups who haven't received new funding in the last year, since there is no obvious sign that internal advocacy is urgently needed there at the present.

Specific job posting websites exist for my profession. Are those websites better for this step than Indeed.com?

In my experience, Indeed.com tends to work best for most people most of the time, but industry-specific job search engines (like Idealist.com for social impact jobs and AngelList for start-ups) may offer more guidance for the families of jobs available in that industry.

If you have doubts, investigate it this way: Find a few interesting postings on your industry-specific website and cross-check them with Indeed.com. If Indeed.com finds everything you found, stay with it. However, if it missed any critical postings or if the alternative site's search guidance proves helpful, feel free to use that instead for this step.

Remember that the goal for this step is to *estimate the urgency* of getting in touch with a particular target based on their current hiring activity, so whichever website best helps you accomplish this is the one you should go with.

Indeed.com didn't find any postings for one of my targets, but that target has job postings on its website! What gives?

Sadly, this does happen occasionally. Neither Indeed.com nor any other job search engine is perfect. Job search engines essentially use Google in tandem with their own methodologies to look for postings featuring your search

continued

terms. However, Google itself requires that a website meet some minimum threshold of popularity and a semblance of traditional structure before it will be "found." Thus, if one or more of your target employers are not heavily trafficked online, Indeed.com may not add a lot of value.

This is absolutely fine for right now, though! We are just assessing whether the employer has any *easy-to-find* postings. If it doesn't, but we later determine that an employer is a top target, we'll find those relevant postings (for example, on the employer's own modest but functional website) soon enough.

Indeed.com doesn't seem to find any results for any of my targets, so my P column is full of 1s—should I try other websites?

If Indeed.com is not returning what you consider a satisfactory number of results, I wouldn't try searching again on a different job search engine. Doing so usually exceeds the *point of diminishing returns*—a term for when results achieved from additional effort simply aren't worth the time and energy required.

Some professions, like law and private equity, tend not to post a lot of jobs in the first place—thus most of your results for the P column may be 1s. But even if only 5 to 10 percent of your targets are hiring right now, that information is crucial for helping you create your order of attack. Others may be hiring right now, but it's better to start with the firms you're **certain** are hiring right now or are at least getting flooded with interest from job seekers because they are advertising openings.

Even if none of your targets have relevant postings, at worst, you are out fifteen minutes of time if you stay disciplined. You'll also have some peace of mind that no one on your employer list is being disproportionately targeted by other job searchers right now.

Part 1: Prioritize Wrap-Up

Your LAMP list is now completely filled in, but you must take a moment to finalize it before moving forward. First, you're going to sort your list again. To do this in your spreadsheet, follow these steps:

1. Highlight your entire LAMP list (L, A, M, and P columns—leave the row numbers out of the sort).

2. Select Sort (which is often located in a drop-down menu called Data or Tools). This brings up a window that asks which criteria you would like to sort your list by. Set your priorities in this order:

(a) Top-level priority: Sorting the M column's values, from largest to smallest—meaning that your 3s, or dream employers, will be at the top of your LAMP list.

(b) Second-level priority: Sorting the P column's values, from largest to smallest. (In some software packages, you'll need to "add a level" of sort prioritization to do this.) This identifies which employers are most time-sensitive.

(c) Third-level priority: Sorting the A column's values in reverse alphabetical order. This means that if all other information is equal, employers with Ys in their A column will be listed before those with Ns.

The final version of your Sort dialog box should look like this before clicking OK (image taken from Microsoft Excel):

continued

Following those steps gives you a sorted LAMP list that looks like this:

#	LIST	ADVOCACY	MOTIVATION	POSTING
1	BiffCo	Y	3	3
2	Staypuft Marshmallow Inc.	N	3	3
3	Darlington Electronics	Y	3	2
4	Ace Tomato Co.	Y	3	1
5	Hanso Corporation	Y	2	3
...	...	...	...	...
...	...	...	...	...
...	...	...	...	...
39	Initech	Y	0	3
40	Zamunda Airlines	N	0	1

This sorting helps us with our second housekeeping task: order verification. The goal of the LAMP process is to give you an ordered list of targets so that your most important and promising employers were addressed first—thus, if you had time to approach only five, you'd be approaching the Top 5 on your list; if you had time to approach only ten, you'd approach the Top 10 on your list; and so on.

Job seekers who don't make a LAMP list tend to start with intuition and finish with intuition when making a target employer list. This results in a short list of obvious, well-known employers that are the same as everyone else's target employers within that space. Instead of starting and finishing with intuition, 2HJS users start with data and finish with intuition. To do this, we verify our list in three different places.

First, look at employer #6 on your list. This is the first employer you will *not* reach out to in your initial batch of outreach, because you'll only be able to start with five employers simultaneously. Does this bother you? If so, is there one of your Top 5 you'd prefer to move down into the sixth spot to make room for your current #6? If so, award your sixth-place employer a Motivation score of 4 and re-sort your list so that it jumps to the top.

Second, look at your top-rated employers with a Motivation score of 2. Are they in your Top 5? If so, you may skip this particular verification step (as we would with Hanso Corporation in our example, since it is our highest-rated employer with a Motivation score of 2 but it is located at #5 in our list). However, if they are outside your Top 5, ask yourself (honestly, now)—does knowing that these employers are advertising a job that is both current and relevant increase your motivation to approach them? If so, increase your Motivation score to reflect your newfound motivation, provided the new information your LAMP list reveals about those employers means you have an increased willingness to apply networking effort toward them. This moves those employers higher on your list.

This may feel like cheating, but the important thing is that we anchored ourselves with *data* before factoring in our intuition—this reduces our risk of creating an overly obvious target employer list.

Third and finally, let's review the employers at the bottom of our list—namely, those we awarded a Motivation score of 0 to because we were not familiar with them. *Now* is when we research those unfamiliar employers, but only selectively—we only research those that are worth our time, specifically because we have an advocate there or because they have a current online job posting that looks interesting. For each one, Google it and *quickly* learn what you can to see if it deserves a higher Motivation score. Usually, that will be ample time for you to learn the basics: its location, industry, products, and so on.

From our example LAMP list, Initech would be one that we'd want to spend a minute or two Googling since it had a Motivation score of 0 but a Posting score of 3 (for a very relevant posting). In that short time, you may learn that Initech is an educational entertainment software company based in Austin, Texas. If you know you could never live in Austin because it's way too hot or too far from your family, change your Motivation score for Initech from a 0 to a 1 and re-sort your list, now that you know enough to be uninterested. Doing so will keep it at

continued

the bottom of your LAMP list, since an employer's Motivation score is its single most important score for determining its LAMP list position.

However, if you could get behind living in Austin, and educational entertainment software sounds interesting to you, change your Motivation score for Initech from a 0 to a 2, a 3, or even a 4, and it will jump to the top of your list. The great thing about initially unknown employers is, the harder you have to look to discover they exist, the less competition there's likely to be for them, meaning that each minute of effort you put toward them brings you greater returns than each minute spent on employers accustomed to getting contacted by job seekers.

After each Motivation score change, re-sort your list (again, by Motivation, Posting, and Advocacy, in that order). Once your Top 5 look like your genuine Top 5 based on all data currently available to you, and employers #6, #7, and #8 look good, but not good enough to replace any of your Top 5, you're done with your LAMP list!

From here on out, your LAMP list provides the game plan you follow for the rest of the process—at least until your job search goals change, if they do (at which point you'd make a new LAMP list). Your LAMP list has identified your Top 5 targets—the ones you'll be reaching out to in Part 2: Contact (chapters 5 to 7). Its job is done.

And with that, I have some great news to share—you've just completed the hardest step of 2HJS! You've opened your mind to what you want next out of life and to an organized process for getting yourself there. Your stress over the design of your job search is over—from here on out, it's just implementation.

I always feel a bit of a rush when I sort a LAMP list—even other people's LAMP lists!—just because it turns anxiety into answers. It stops being data and starts being a story that's about to be written. I hope you enjoyed watching your list snap into place. Please do take a moment to celebrate how far you've come.

LIST	ADVOCACY	MOTIVATION	POSTING
✓	✓	✓	✓

TROUBLESHOOTING

Shouldn't I practice outreach on backup employers before approaching my genuine Top 5?

Absolutely not! Too often when I see job seekers take this approach, their backup employers are so flattered and impressed by the job seeker's proactivity and gumption that they quickly make an offer, putting the job seeker in an incredibly difficult situation—accept an offer from a backup without ever knowing if a dream employer would have been interested, or decline that bird-in-the-hand offer in order to pursue the two-in-the-bush dream employers. It's brutal, and I see it happen again and again.

Thankfully, there is a natural bias in LAMP lists toward better-known and larger employers, and these employers tend to have the longest lead times when hiring. This means that you need to start networking at these sooner than at smaller organizations, where hiring tends to be more just-in-time in nature.

Another benefit of having larger employers at the top of your list is that it gives you more people within your dream firms to practice on with minimal risk. Even if your first informational meeting is a bit awkward, your contacts have better things to do than send mass emails banning you from any further consideration to the rest of their colleagues! More likely, they'll just forget they spoke to you entirely before the day is over, and you'll begin anew with someone else tomorrow!

#### PART 2

Contact:
Boosters, Obligates,
and Curmudgeons

NATURALIZE

What do you mean by "Naturalize"?

In this chapter, I'll teach you how to "create" contacts at your Top 5 employers, even if you have no existing contacts or other connections there.

Naturalization typically refers to the process by which someone becomes a citizen of a country by means other than birth, but more generally the term means "to gain admittance to a new community." In 2HJS, to *naturalize* means to (1) identify and (2) find contact information for potential advocates who are most likely to help us gain admittance into their professional network.

Incidentally, naturalizing contacts is *absolutely* my favorite step to help job seekers with. At heart, it is a refreshing bit of amateur detective work, and you'll be amazed (and likely a bit disturbed) at how much you can learn about people these days armed only with the internet, a systematic approach, and a bit of creativity.

Why is a systematic approach to creating contacts even necessary?

While you have been creating contacts (literally) your entire life, you've likely never had to do so in such a premeditated fashion and with such high stakes.

Furthermore, the goal isn't making a sale or a new friend, but finding advocates capable of influencing employee selection at their organizations. That's a pretty specialized case, so a pretty specialized approach becomes appropriate, especially when your time, energy, and pain tolerance for learning to job search is quite limited. That's where the next step of 2HJS, Part 2: Contact, comes into play.

In this chapter we discuss how to ascertain the identities and contact information of promising contacts at each of our Top 5 LAMP list employers, and in the two subsequent chapters in Part 2 we examine how to write and send highly efficient correspondence (Chapter 6: The 6-Point Email) and manage a lot of simultaneous outreach without becoming overwhelmed or forgetful (Chapter 7: Track).

In total, Part 2: Contact will take 50 minutes, broken down as follows:

CHAPTER #	TIME REQUIRED
Chapter 5: Naturalize	20 minutes
Chapter 6: The 6-Point Email	20 minutes
Chapter 7: Track	10 minutes
Total for Part 2: Contact	50 minutes

With those steps completed, we will secure one or more informational meetings with our targeted contacts. We'll cover how to prepare, conduct, and follow-up on those conversations to get interviews in the final part, Part 3: Convince.

Isn't naturalizing contacts *now* inefficient? Why didn't we find and log these contacts during the Advocacy column step?

Had we tried to Naturalize contacts during Part 1 where we made our LAMP list, we would have wasted a lot of time searching for contacts we would never use at employers we frankly don't care that much about.

The crucial difference between then and now is that now we know which five employers are worth our additional time and effort. Our LAMP list gives us this precise information.

We're effectively co-opting the airline industry's discovery from the 1980s that not all of their customers were equally profitable. Treating certain ones better than others was actually very profitable, and establishing frequent flier programs allowed the airlines to more quickly recognize which customers deserved greater investment. These investments ranged from material perks like complimentary business-class upgrades to service advantages like early boarding.

Our LAMP list has basically helped us determine who our "most-valued customers" are. We devote our valuable time and energy to targeting *them* before the others lower on our list, and the first thing we need to do is to identify our two most promising contacts (whom I call "starter contacts") for each of our Top 5 employers.

Wait, *two* contacts? Won't one suffice?

Sometimes, but not typically. You may find this surprising, but it turns out that not everyone responds to job seekers' outreach emails! Who knew, right?

In fact, response rates to your 6-Point Emails (which I'll teach you about in the next chapter) average between 20 and 40 percent, meaning every time you send one out, you are more likely to get ignored than you are to get a response.

The good news is that the people who reply to 6-Point Emails are disproportionately the right kind of contact, a topic we also explore in more detail in chapter 6. However, since we'll likely get ignored by at least one person at each of our Top 5 employers, it makes sense to identify two starter contacts rather than one so we're ready to go in case the first person proves unhelpful. (Should we need third, fourth, or even tenth contacts, we can go back to find those people later as needed; we discuss this more in chapter 7.)

So how do we identify these starter contacts?

The short answer is "systematically," just like everything else in this process. Starter contacts can be found for *any* employer, once we've decided they are a priority—the challenge is to find one efficiently. Thankfully, LinkedIn's custom search (see Technology Corner #2 on page 39) makes this pretty easy, even if you do not have a premium membership or a large number of existing contacts.

I recommend the following hierarchy of traits for identifying starter contacts for each of our Top 5, in order of importance:

Trait #1: Their position is functionally relevant to the one you are seeking.

Trait #2: They are fellow alumni or members of your preferred affinity group.

Trait #3: They hold a position one to two levels above where you would start.

Trait #4: They have already been promoted at that organization.

Trait #5: They have a unique name.

This marks a departure from the original edition of this book. After thousands of iterations of this process, I have found that I had to reverse the order of the top two criteria, since functional relevance (Trait #1) has proved to be a stronger predictor of whether a contact will be helpful than being a fellow "alumni" (Trait #2). Note that in this book, I use the term *alumni* without quotation marks to describe literal alumni—people who attended the same school(s) you did—and I use the "alumni" in quotation marks to describe both literal alumni and fellow members of nondegree affinity groups, such as the military veteran community, nondegree training programs, and colleagues from your home country.

This difference in predictive ability is attributable to two factors: first, informational meetings with people outside your job function of interest are more likely to be awkward (and therefore less likely to result in referrals) because you don't understand their line of work very well and vice versa; and second, even if the conversation goes smoothly, the "alum" doesn't know who to refer you to next, since they are less familiar with key recruiting influencers in your desired job function than they are with their own.

To actually identify a functionally relevant contact, enter a job title keyword (like "manager," "engineer," or "finance") into the Title field and click Apply to produce a list of candidates. If you have many options, screen it for alumni by adding your schools attended to the Schools field in LinkedIn's custom search screen, and once again click Apply to see whether any potential starter contacts match your criteria. Sadly, LinkedIn provides no standard way to search for figurative "alumni," like fellow LinkedIn Group members, but previous 2HJS users have identified some clever approaches to approximating this (see sidebar, page 91).

That said, resist the urge to click on many individual profiles to ascertain this information (see Time Out #5, page 90).

When selecting functionally relevant contacts, you may have many "alumni" (or none at all), in which case you'd try to break the tie by next identifying which of your remaining candidates are one to two levels above the position where you would start in the company (Trait #3). Targeting people one to two levels above you is the "Goldilocks zone," meaning that they are neither too senior nor too junior. However, if your only remaining candidates are either very senior or very junior, opt for the more senior contacts over the more junior ones. Even if they are too busy to speak to you, senior contacts can refer you to a subordinate, incidentally making that subordinate *very* motivated to help you. A junior employee unfortunately can't refer you to senior personnel if they're too busy, despite their potentially greater empathy for your plight.

Time Out #5

Click at Your Own Risk!

It may seem logical that a great way to identify potential contacts is to view *many* profiles to identify those with whom you have hometowns, affinities, LinkedIn Groups, or other similarities in common. However, avoid this temptation because it may result in LinkedIn identifying you as a potential executive recruiter, which means you will have search limits imposed on you each calendar month—the only solution for which is to wait until the next calendar month or upgrade to an expensive recruiter-level LinkedIn subscription.

In particular, one of the quickest ways to hit this search limit seems to be by clicking the profiles that appear in the People Also Viewed box within any individual profile within LinkedIn. So whatever you do, don't fall down the rabbit hole of clicking profiles randomly.

Following proper 2HJS technique, where you only click in people's profiles once you have narrowed the possibilities down to a handful of candidates—and only for your current Top 5 employers from your LAMP list—you will not hit this limit. It just takes a little discipline.

Unfortunately, employers don't typically publish their organizational charts, so you'll have to approximate their level based on their current job title listed in LinkedIn. Don't worry about being perfect here; an 80/20 Rule approach is totally appropriate for this task. In general, managers oversee analysts and associates, while principals and directors oversee managers and are in turn overseen by vice presidents, who report to the CEO/CFO/president/and so on.

By now we should have narrowed the starter contact field down to a few people (less than ten), so clicking on individual

"Alumni" Search Workarounds

Users have found a number of workarounds when searching for figurative "alumni," which are difficult to find within LinkedIn's custom search interface.

International job seekers: International job seekers tend to find that fellow professionals from their home countries are disproportionately helpful. My two favorite approaches for international job seekers are to search either via their native language (if different than where they are job searching) or for alumni of other major universities from their home country.

Military veterans: Military veterans also find fellow veterans to be disproportionately helpful when job searching. There is no way to search veterans directly via LinkedIn, but there is a LinkedIn Group called the Veteran Mentor Network, the single largest veteran-related LinkedIn Group with well over 100,000 members, which provides some infrastructure for finding fellow veterans, including a link that auto-populates a list of branches of the military in the Previous Company field on LinkedIn's custom search page.

profiles to identify candidates who have been internally promoted (Trait #4) becomes feasible without triggering LinkedIn search limits. Internally promoted candidates—namely, those who have held multiple job titles within the organization, according to their LinkedIn profile—are the best contacts to approach for two reasons: first, they know more about how to effectively navigate the recruiting scene at their firm due to their tenure than someone who just joined six months ago, for example; and second, they have more social capital and confidence to leverage when advocating for a job seeker than a contact still working toward a first promotion who has not yet been assured by colleagues and management that their work is widely valued.

As a final tiebreaker, I recommend picking uniquely named contacts (Trait #5), since you may need to try and figure out their professional email address at some point. It is easier to guess the work email address belonging to someone with an uncommon name than it is to sort through countless duplicates.

Still with me? Great! Now that we've identified our two starter contacts for each of our Top 5 employers from our LAMP list, let's find their contact information!

Let me guess—you've got a hierarchy for finding contact information too?

Heck yeah I do. Here it is:

Contact method #1: LinkedIn Groups

Contact method #2: Direct email

    a. Alumni database

    b. Email finders

    c. "Fan mail"

Contact method #3: LinkedIn invitations to connect

Contact method #4: Facebook/Twitter/other social media

Contact method #5: LinkedIn second-degree connections

As we go lower on the list, the average rate of return on effort decreases, and we want to use the method with the highest average rate of return available to us at any given time.

What is an average rate of return?

An *average rate of return* is the amount of benefit you expect to gain per unit of investment (be it time, money, or even attention). For example, imagine that you and I play a game in which you would pay me $1 every time a 1, 2, 3, 4, or 5 was rolled on a fair, six-sided die, but every time a 6 came up I would pay you $10,000. If we played this dice game six hundred times, on average, you would win one hundred times (for a profit of a cool $1 million!) and lose five hundred times (for a loss of $500) for an average profit of $999,500. If we played this game just six times, on average you would win once (for a profit of $10,000) and lose five times (for a loss of $5), yielding a profit of $9,995. However, the average rate of return would not change, even though your profits would. Specifically, the average rate of return refers to the average outcome per game, no matter how many times you play (be it six hundred, six million, or just once).

What does average rate of return have to do with how I find my starter contacts?

Each of the contact methods I listed earlier requires different amounts of time and effort to execute, and that time and effort is part of the average-rate-of-return calculation. For example, "fan mail," which you'll learn about shortly, has perhaps the highest success rate in terms of getting a response, but it requires significantly more time and uncertainty than the methods ranked above it. As a result, fan mail's average rate of return per minute of job search time is lower than the methods above it, making it a better backup option than a primary option.

Now let's discuss each of the methods in descending order of their average rate of return.

CONTACT METHOD #1: LINKEDIN GROUPS

As I wrote earlier, LinkedIn Groups are the best-kept secret in the job search. If you share a LinkedIn Group with a LinkedIn contact, you may message that person directly for free through that LinkedIn Group but only if you know how to access this information correctly. For a refresher, see "What are LinkedIn Groups?" on page 38. (Note that this functionality may change as LinkedIn updates its offerings, so if this technique no longer works, please visit this book's LinkedIn Group, "The 2-Hour Job Search—Q&A Forum," for more info).

The key is to look up your starter contact in the LinkedIn Group's directory rather than through LinkedIn's main search or custom search. As a reminder, join any and all alumni LinkedIn groups you can access as well as any related to your general interests. Interest-based groups are especially powerful if you do not attend college or have worked for smaller employers.

As of this printing, you can belong to up to a hundred groups at one time, so don't be shy! Target larger groups that match your interests, since they give you direct email access to more people. It will typically take a few days for you to be approved for these groups, and LinkedIn will make you wait four days before you can message fellow group members, so join groups now so they will be active by the time you are ready to launch your outreach.

Once you have access to a LinkedIn Group you share with a starter contact, navigate to that group's LinkedIn page and click on the number of members in that group. This takes you to a directory of fellow group members and a search box. Look up your starter contact's name there, and when they pop up, you'll see you have a new messaging option next to their name—click on that option, and you'll be able to send them a note directly, no email address required! You don't even need to supply a subject line to your email—LinkedIn provides that for you ("New message from <your name> in <Group name>")—so even less work!

Not everyone checks their LinkedIn mail regularly, but those who do tend to be disproportionately helpful. We discuss these different types of contacts in more detail in chapter 6.

CONTACT METHOD #2: DIRECT EMAIL

The second-best average rate of return on your outreach will come from emailing starter contacts directly at their professional (or voluntarily offered personal) email addresses.

The best method for finding direct email addresses is an alumni database, when applicable. In such databases, alumni will provide direct email addresses on occasion—sometimes professional ones and sometimes personal ones. Feel free to use either, as they have been furnished for fellow alumni's use. One caveat: This information can fall out of date. When people change jobs they tend to update LinkedIn profiles but not necessarily alumni database(s); so if you see outdated employer or email address information (such as an email ending in @mindspring.com), consider a different option!

The second-best method for finding direct email addresses is through the use of email-finding websites. These websites typically offer two different services: email formulation and email testing. For email formulation, you can enter a company's website domain and it will "scrape" the internet to find email addresses associated with that domain, often suggesting what it thinks the email convention is at that firm with surprising accuracy. For email testing, you can enter your guess at a person's professional email address, and the website will "ping" the address to see if an email would go through to it.

My current favorite email finder is Hunter (www.hunter.io). Hunter offers you both email formulation and email verification for free if you register an email address, and it gives you additional detail that increases your return on effort—specifically, whether a particular web domain accepts all emails sent to anything ending in their suffix (meaning you wouldn't receive a bounce-back email if you email an incorrect address).

The third-best method for finding email addresses is "fan mail," an inherently creative and scrappy approach to finding email addresses. It gets its name from its original inspiration in the pre-internet days, where the best way to get in touch with famous people was to write them letters to ask them why they're so good at their job. In our context, "fan mail" means . . . basically the same thing. You read an interesting article about or by someone in your line of work and you reach out to ask them if they're willing to share why they are so good at their job (the easiest informational meeting of all!).

The only thing people enjoy talking about more than themselves is their media appearances, so when this method is based on a media citation, it tends to result in very high response rates! However, it is also the most speculative approach, meaning it has one of the lowest returns on effort given the time it takes to find appropriate articles and then find a person's direct email address (or vice versa when targeting smaller employers). Thus, save it for tiny employers and/or very senior contacts, as those categories of contacts tend to appear in the media most frequently.

Other resources that may also assist you in finding fan mail–based email addresses include the contact's LinkedIn profile (note that some people on LinkedIn list direct emails in their About or Contact Info sections), at the end of articles written by the contact, the employer's own website (best for contacts at small employers, who often list all employees individually in their About Us page), conference presentation abstracts, and financial disclosures (best for very senior contacts).

Note that a maximum of five minutes should be spent trying to employ this method for a particular contact. If no email address is found within that period of time, you should move to a customized LinkedIn invitation to connect.

CONTACT METHOD #3: LINKEDIN INVITATIONS TO CONNECT

The third-best average rate of return on your outreach comes from (customized) LinkedIn invitations to connect. This is the easiest way to contact potential advocates since you can reach most anyone directly with a minimum amount of time and effort. But the response rates can be lower given it's a rather forward way to introduce yourself—you know, by asking a stranger to make a permanent, public connection with you for the remainder of your internet lives. (Granted, there *is* a way to respond to connection requests without accepting the request, but it's best never to bet on others' ability to grasp technological nuance. . . .) However, this is a fine approach when used sparingly and when another means for reaching out to your contact has not presented itself using the previous methods within a few minutes of effort.

If you *do* use this method, be sure to customize your request to follow the 6-Point Email framework we discuss in the next chapter to maximize your response rates.

CONTACT METHOD #4: FACEBOOK/TWITTER/OTHER SOCIAL MEDIA

True, Facebook, Twitter, and Instagram are more social networking websites than professional ones, but their long odds of success are counteracted by the minimal effort required and potential gigantic payoff. Essentially, this step involves asking your friends whether they know anyone at those Top 5 target employers for which you've been unable to locate starter contacts so far.

This takes mere seconds, but it could give you exactly what you're looking for. However, you should use this strategy judiciously; use it too frequently (daily or several times a week) and you could alienate your friends and/or followers. Thus you want to first make sure there are no obvious contacts you're overlooking.

That said, using Facebook or Twitter during the Naturalization process makes use of a concept identified by Stanford sociologist professor Mark Granovetter. He called it "the strength of weak ties" in a paper he authored back in 1973—decades before Facebook and Twitter emerged.[1] The theory behind the strength of weak ties is that very close friends tend to share social networks, making them relatively redundant in the world of the job search. Furthermore, LinkedIn, being primarily a tool for professionals, links people in similar professions more frequently than not—again, causing social networks to overlap.

You may be connected to your weaker ties—your theater-major college roommate who now designs sets on Broadway, for example—on Facebook (a *social* network) but not on LinkedIn (a *professional* network). However, your ex-roommate's social network is likely to be *entirely* different from yours, given how much your lives have diverged over the last few years. Thus this "weak tie" is more likely than your closest friends to have a relevant contact you haven't already uncovered, and that person may be willing to give you a ringing endorsement due to the formative life experiences you shared. Similarly, that nice person you chatted with on an airplane, whom you expected never to see or hear from again but later found on Facebook, has an entirely different social network and may likewise be willing to connect you.

The strength of weak ties is a powerful concept in the job search—you simply never know. Thus a simple status update of, "Can anyone put me in touch with someone from Darlington Electronics? In marketing, if possible?" could result in several offers, as it is a wonderful chance to quickly reconnect and help a friend move forward in life. Altruism, a social norm rather than a market norm (and a concept that forms the backbone of chapter 6), is a powerful motivator.

The return on effort here has the potential to be massive—a relevant connection can be found in just seconds. However, because this option is exhaustible, you should save it for situations when the more common approaches have failed.

I'm not currently on Facebook or Twitter? Do I need to join or become active again for job search purposes?

No. They are the devil. If you're not already using social media, just pick a new contact or try again to use one of the previous methods rather than investing time and effort into a speculative approach. Don't forget that you can also post status updates on LinkedIn, so that would be one last weak-tie network option to try before trying an even more speculative approach.

CONTACT METHOD #5: LINKEDIN SECOND-DEGREE CONNECTIONS

Last and definitely least, we have second-degree connections. "But wait, Steve," you might be thinking. "Aren't second-degree connections why we joined LinkedIn in the first place?" Yes, they were, but the longer you're on LinkedIn, they less useful they become, as an ever-increasing majority of your first-degree connections fall out of date.

With contacts that have fallen out of date, it would be rude to cite them as a reference without mentioning to them that you would be doing so. (Note that this is fine if your mutual connection is someone you keep up with—in practice for 2HJS purposes, I define this as someone you could send an email or text message to and expect a prompt response back.) You would therefore have to first reestablish a connection with that person. However, it would *also* be rude to reach out to someone for the first time in a decade only to ask if you could use their name in a job search email, so you'd want to try to reestablish a social connection with them before asking for their professional assistance, and so on.

The funny thing is that it also may have been a decade since *your* connection spoke to your desired contact! That's the problem with second-degree connections—too often it's two degrees of stranger, and success via this route means getting the help of two people instead of just one. That results in a terrible average rate of return, so I recommend skipping this approach if you have any other approach available to you.

And with that, we are done with the Naturalize step of Part 2! Thus, it is now time to move on to the next step—emailing our newly found contacts. Prepare for liftoff!

TROUBLESHOOTING

What if someone from my past works at one of my Top 5 employers? How do I get them to help me?

Unfortunately, as with all of the job search, there is no way to control outcomes, only process. It seems intuitive that "having a connection" at a Top 5 employer would be helpful, but if that connection is not a current one, I typically find this path to be more trouble and disappointment than it is worth.

It's counterintuitive, but *it is actually far more difficult to change the urgency of an existing contact than to establish an urgent connection with a brand-new contact.* Once someone knows you in a nonurgent context—for example, you attended college with them many years ago but haven't kept in touch or you met this person at a conference a few years ago or they are a distant family member—it's very difficult

continued

in practice to get them to suddenly prioritize your job search out of nowhere.

Thus, attempt to reinvigorate your existing contacts by seeing if they are open to a social outreach, but if they prove resistant to being helpful, know that this is normal. The great news is 2HJS works best with total strangers. Why? Because strangers are predictable. They respond to outreach from job seekers in one of three very predictable ways, which we outline in the next chapter. Thus, even if you have zero connections on LinkedIn or relevant industry contacts in your life already, you are still as qualified to succeed from implementing 2HJS as anyone else is!

What if I know (or think I know) who the hiring manager for the position is based on the profiles I find in LinkedIn—I should automatically start with that person, right?

Tread carefully here. I'd still advise you to follow the recommended hierarchy. If you've found a job posting and the hiring manager's name is listed directly on it, I'd say choose someone else—at least initially. Yes, going to them directly would ensure you are on their radar before they make a decision, but that person's inbox becomes its own version of an online job posting, flooded with applicants and information seekers alike who want to "learn more about the open position." Going to a clearly identified hiring manager directly is like going to HR directly when you are not interested in an HR position, meaning this person is not functionally relevant. Due to the high volume of inquiries they receive, they will focus only on "perfect fit" candidates initially and put the rest on the back burner, perhaps indefinitely. If the hiring manager's name is NOT readily available, feel free to reach out directly. Their volume of inbound interest is unlikely to be as high, and they may be willing to help.

The better play is to approach someone else in or near that work group (as best you can surmise, at least) and try to develop a relationship with *them*. They are not getting the same level of inbound traffic, so they may be open to actually getting to know you a bit. If they like you and choose to hand you off to the hiring manager, the hiring manager will be much nicer to you and easier to work with since you have been prevalidated.

Second-degree informational interviews that directly result from a referral made in a previous informational, are *much* easier conversations. They tend to focus much more explicitly on getting you in the pipeline for a screening interview. You will find the reception you receive to be warmer and the content of the conversation to be more future job interview related.

What if I'm interested in a particular group within a much larger company? Can I find that in LinkedIn?

This is indeed possible, but it requires a slightly different approach. Let's say you are especially interested in one particular imprint of a larger publishing company. Unfortunately, that imprint's name won't appear in the Current Companies field of LinkedIn's custom search since it is just a division of the larger publishing company, but if you look for the larger publishing company, you get contacts from all the other imprints mixed in.

To find contacts in this situation, leave the parent company's name in the Current Employer field, but add the subsidiary's name in the free-response Company field at the bottom of the custom search page. This field does not auto-complete for you, so you need to be sure your spelling is correct (and use quotes if it is a multiword name); but by searching in this manner, you will be able to find contacts that mention the subsidiary somewhere in their employer descriptions.

## CHAPTER 6

THE 6-POINT EMAIL

20 MINUTES

Quickstart Exercise #2A

Sell Yourself

Imagine one of your dream employers. Next, imagine the job title of the person you'd most like to speak to at this employer. For real—take all the time you need, as this concept is brutally important to all of your progress going forward. Got it? Okay, here's the exercise.

In the next thirty seconds, mentally draft an outreach email to this person in which you "sell yourself" to try to convince them to do an informational meeting with you. Write down key points if you find it helpful.

All done? Make a note of how this task felt. Was it easy and comfortable? Or was it difficult and uncomfortable? In either case, why do you think it felt that way?

We'll revisit this exercise a bit later in the chapter in Quickstart Exercise #2B on page 109.

How does a 6-Point Email differ from any other outreach-oriented email?

The 6-Point Email is shorter, simpler, and more efficient than other outreach emails since it specifically targets those contacts that are most likely to provide you with real help in the job search. A job seeker need only keep six points in mind to create such an email. In this chapter, I'll teach you to do exactly that.

I think by now I know how to email people for job search help—it's getting them to write me *back* that's the problem. So how do I do that?

This is the million-dollar question—and by far the most common complaint I hear from job seekers about the search process: "People never write me back." And I agree with them—no matter how customized your outreach, how similar your backgrounds, or how relevant your abilities, some contacts will never write you back.

And that's okay. As you'll find out later, those who ignore you are actually doing you a favor. It's the people who pretend to be helpful that are dangerous. The key is to target the helpful kind of contacts in your outreach, and that is what the 6-Point Email was invented to do.

So, level with me—is this chapter going to tell me anything I don't already know?

Absolutely. In fact, employing 2HJS effectively requires forgetting everything you've ever learned about networking with strangers, because technology has now rendered the long-standing conventional wisdom on this topic—"sell yourself"—wrong and counterproductive.

Technology has fundamentally changed the way we interact with information. In the early days of email, back when spam only referred to a manufactured meat product, every email would actually be read. Today we seem to spend more time cleaning out our inboxes than we do responding or writing new messages. Instead of reading, as people used to, we now filter. If you want proof, pull up one of your favorite websites and see what's going on, just as you normally would.

Now that you've skimmed the page in your usual fashion, go back and look at the page again. I mean *really* look at it. The first time, did you even notice the banner ad at the top? The suggested purchases on the right? The various headers you rarely click on under the website's name? We ignore the vast majority of information we encounter—and outreach emails we receive from job seekers are no exception.

Although job search technology has changed so much—thirty years ago, could we imagine the online job applications and job search engines that exist today?—the conventional wisdom has not changed, despite the fact that there is so much more info distracting us these days. Therein lies the problem.

According to a 2017 Symantec report, 54 percent of all email sent in the first half of that year was spam. Thus over half of emails you receive should rightfully be ignored. Thankfully, email filters catch many of those these days, but we are still inundated by emails from people and organizations we *do* know. If your name isn't recognized by the recipient, your content needs to get to the point quickly. Spending precious words discussing your previous experience or including hyperlinks to other websites will likely result in your email getting deleted unread, especially in an era when more and more emails are being read on mobile devices with screens designed for no more than a hundred words at a time.

Therefore, in this chapter we're going to completely redesign the "traditional" outreach email and rebuild it from the ground up into something leaner, more efficient, and more effective. A key piece to making this possible is the recognition that all potential contacts are not created equal—some will be far more helpful than others. To maximize our efficiency, therefore, we need to target the right customer segment of contacts with the right kind of email.

What is a customer segment?

A *customer segment* is a subset of a population of customers (in this case, all potential contacts we may reach out to for help) that share characteristics in the way they interact with and consume a certain product. During my marketing days at General Mills, I learned that Cheerios had two distinct customer segments: new parents and health-conscious adults.

New parents buy Cheerios as a way to love and nurture their children. For many of these new parents, Cheerios were their own first solid food, so it becomes a tradition that gets handed down through generations. Adding to their appeal for the new parent segment, Cheerios are highly portable—easy to put in a resealable plastic bag for on-the-go eating—and should any spills happen, they are simple to clean up. Plus, most young children really enjoy the taste and the fun "O" shape.

However, health-conscious adults couldn't care less about the easy cleanup and "O" shape. That customer segment buys Cheerios for a very different reason: to reduce their cholesterol. On its box, Cheerios points out that its soluble fiber content is clinically proven to help reduce a person's cholesterol as part of a heart-healthy diet.

These two target customer segments buy Cheerios for totally different reasons, but the result is the same: purchase. Thus, commercials targeting the new parent segment may focus on the nurturing aspect of the product, whereas ads for cholesterol-concerned consumers may focus on its health benefits instead.

Okay, so how does knowing about customer segments help me email potential job search contacts?

First, it alerts you to the fact that job search contacts can be segmented just as Cheerios shoppers can. Different segments of contacts respond to your outreach differently because each has different values and motivations—therefore, expecting all of them to respond to an outreach email in a similar fashion is unrealistic.

Through my experience over the years, I've identified three main segments of job search contacts. We discuss each of these segments in turn, starting with the one I mentioned at the beginning of this chapter.

If you recall, I agreed wholeheartedly that there is a segment of contacts who will never write you back, no matter how personalized your email to them is. I call this segment *Curmudgeons*. Curmudgeons are awful people. They hate babies, kick puppies, floss at their desks, and so on. Or, Curmudgeons are wonderful people who simply have no interest in helping you find a job. It honestly makes no difference; they are ignoring you!

Oddly, though, Curmudgeons are actually not the worst segment of contacts. At least they don't hide the fact they won't be helpful—unlike *Obligates*, our second (and worst) segment of contacts.

Whereas Curmudgeons are motivated by self-interest (in terms of time, emotional investment, or any other number of factors), Obligates are motivated by guilt. Perhaps they benefited from the help of others when getting their last job, so now they feel *obligated* to do the same for someone else, for example. However, they certainly don't want to do so (by definition), so they try to do just enough to save face and get on with their day.

Obligates are the worst segment because the average rate of return is negative, rather than zero as it is with Curmudgeons. With Curmudgeons, you know within a couple of quick formulaic emails that they won't respond, so, although you get no results, you've lost very little time and energy. Obligates, on the other hand, tend to consume *significant* amounts of your time and effort before revealing that they won't be very helpful. Perhaps they take a week to respond to your outreach email or they need weeks to schedule an informational meeting with you or they ask for questions in advance so they can answer via email rather than form a relationship with you or they cancel that informational meeting at the last minute and then suddenly become very squirrelly about rescheduling with you.

The net result is that you as a job seeker spend a lot of time trying to connect with someone who doesn't genuinely want to connect with you.

Unfortunately, Obligates frequently send false-positive signals to job seekers. Remember, they are motivated by a sense of obligation, so they don't want the breakdown in the relationship to be perceived as *their* fault. However, they will then take steps to either keep you at arm's length ("I don't have time for an informational meeting, but send me your resume and I'll try to forward it to some people") or slow down the process enough that eventually you'll move on to someone else. Worse still, there is no way to spot them in advance based on their level, LinkedIn profile, tenure, or any other factor.

The 80/20 Rule applies once again in the networking phase of this process, because a vast majority of the help you receive in your job search will come from a minority of people. I call this third and final contact segment *Boosters*. Boosters genuinely enjoy helping people. They're already in before you even ask—they just need you to raise your hand and identify yourself to them.

There's no checkbox on LinkedIn that says, "I'm a Booster! Start here!" or "I'm a Curmudgeon—don't even bother," so in chapter 7, we'll learn how to differentiate between Boosters and Obligates based on their responses to our 6-Point Email, since everything I teach you from this point forward is designed to appeal to Boosters even if it means alienating Obligates and Curmudgeons.

Why would we want to alienate *anyone* in the job search?

I understand this may seem bold or careless, but think about it. Based on what we know, Curmudgeons are never going to write back to us and Obligates provide a negative return on effort. Thus, the fewer Obligates we engage with, the more time we have to find Boosters. Getting a job in an era in which hundreds of resumes get submitted overnight for a new job posting requires genuine human advocacy, and only Boosters provide that.

I know—you've been trained to write outreach emails that attempt to appeal to everyone, but I'm going to help you get more out of your efforts by helping you expressly target Boosters. They give us the highest rate of return—the most payoff with the least effort—so why not?

That said, maximizing our appeal to Boosters in an initial outreach email is a very different (and, thankfully, simpler!) process than writing an outreach email designed for anyone and everyone. To understand how to write such an email (namely, the 6-Point Email that is the crux of this chapter), we must first learn how best to enlist a stranger to help us move a couch.

Let me guess—with lots and lots of money?

Yes. And no. It comes from an experiment conducted by my Fuqua colleague, behavioral economist Dan Ariely, which he outlines in his book *Predictably Irrational*. In his study, an experimenter asked passersby to help them move a couch out of their moving truck under one of three conditions—for no compensation, for a small wage, and for a reasonable wage (such as what you might offer a mover if one were available for immediate hire nearby).

Take a moment and pick which approach you think would be most successful.

Did you guess a reasonable wage? If so, you are correct! Paying someone a reasonable wage for labor is an effective motivator—it's how most capitalist economies generally work, after all.

That said, you might also assume that offering something is better than nothing; however, that's where you'd be wrong. Surprisingly, offering *no* compensation at all was just as effective as offering a reasonable wage, but offering only a small wage was less effective than either of the other scenarios!

Ariely explained that the introduction of compensation into the request shifts the scenario from one based on a social norm (that is, a favor) to one based on a market norm (that is, work-for-hire). Philanthropy, he found, even on such a small scale, could be a very powerful motivator, but once compensation is introduced, *sufficient* money had to be offered to break even with the no-money scenario.

Quickstart Exercise #2B

Ask for a Favor

Recall the dream employer and dream job title you brainstormed in Quickstart Exercise #2A on page 102? For this exercise, I want you to once again mentally draft an outreach email in the next thirty seconds to this contact asking them to speak to you; but instead of selling yourself, ask for a favor. Once again, write down key points if you find it helpful.

All done? How did it feel to write the email this time compared to the "sell yourself" version?

Most attendees of my live sessions find this iteration to be a far more positive experience than the "sell yourself" version for a few different reasons: asking for a favor feels more authentic, causes much less decision anxiety (there are only so many ways to ask for a favor, after all), and requires far fewer words than "selling yourself" does.

Before we move on, ask yourself what about this outreach email seemed to work well.

It's likely you stumbled across a few of the six points we're about to discuss, and all it took was a change in perspective and thirty seconds of effort. The 6-Point Email is a version of what you just brainstormed, except it has been optimized by thousands of job seekers over the course of a dozen years. Relax, grab some popcorn, and enjoy the fruits of other people's labor for a change!

How does this relate to the job search?

Very simply, up to this point, you've likely heard you should network using market norms—"Here's the value I'll bring to your company" and "Here's my background, which you should find compelling." In anything less than a stellar job market where employees get "finder's fees" for bringing in new employees, there is very little chance that anyone you contact will ever personally gain from helping you join their employer. In fact, they actually take a risk by doing so, because if you turn out to be psychotic and make a bad impression on the senior person they hand you off to, their own reputations will suffer for having recommended you.

As Ariely's experiment shows, once you bring compensation into the equation, you have to offer enough for it to be worth someone's while. I'd argue that unless you have experience directly related to the targeted job (and even then), it will be nearly impossible to offer a "reasonable wage" that entices a contact to help you.

The real nugget in the study is the realization that social norms are *powerful*. Better still, they attract the right kind of audience—people who derive genuine joy from helping others: Boosters, in other words.

Because it takes a good deal of money to match the efficacy of offering no money at all in the couch experiment, we adopt the same principle for our outreach. We cut everything about how the employer or employee will benefit from hiring you, and we simply ask for a favor. The 6-Point Email is the most efficient way to ask for the favor of time from Boosters.

So, what exactly is a 6-Point Email?

It is an email requesting an informational meeting, which is written using six key points as guidelines:

Point #1: Write fewer than seventy-five words.

Point #2: Ask for insight and advice, not job leads.

Point #3: State your connection first.

Point #4: Make your request in the form of a question (ending in "?").

Point #5: Define your interest both narrowly and broadly.

Point #6: Keep over half the word count about the *contact*, not about you.

Point #1 may be a bit startling. "Write fewer than seventy-five words?" Indeed, looking over your own previous informational meeting request emails, you may see they are in the two-hundred- to five-hundred-word range. That's simply how many words it takes to employ the conventional wisdom of selling yourself: talking about your background, demonstrating some employer research, guesstimating your value to an employer, and so on. However, that email is likely tedious to read even for you—can you imagine receiving it from someone you don't even know? It would feel like they were trying to tell you why two dollars should be sufficient motivation to help them move a couch!

Please remember that this is not your fault. You have been following well-entrenched conventional wisdom from well-trusted advisers. I myself gave this same counterproductive advice when I first started out!

It took struggling over editing one too many four-hundred-word outreach emails as a career coach before I finally (and ashamedly) admitted, "I really don't want to read this." But if *I* didn't want to read it, and I was getting paid to do so, who *would* want to read it? Unlike me, the intended recipients of these emails did not earn their raises or promotions by helping out job seekers.

During my corporate careers before I became a career coach, I would simply glance at these messages to see whether the sender had a referral from anyone I knew and liked. If I didn't see that in the first few seconds, I would delete it and get back to work, assuming a kinder-hearted colleague would reply in my stead or that the job seeker would follow-up if truly dedicated.

Even generous Boosters with time to burn would be better served by an email more suited to their "help-anyone" attitude. Lengthy outreach emails are a holdover from the envelope-and-stamp days when letters shorter than half a page might seem rude. However, the "kitchen sink" approach of including lots of information you want the recipient to know and hoping enough of it is relevant to warrant a callback simply doesn't work in the short-attention-span age of smartphones and Twitter. Anything more than seventy-five words from a stranger seems downright presumptuous.

Fine, then—show me one of these 6-Point Emails that does it all in fewer than seventy-five words.

A totally fair request. One of my original 2-Hour Job Searchers, Brooke, had completed her LAMP list (back when there was *only* a LAMP list— Parts 2 and 3 didn't exist yet), and she asked me how to maximize her chances of getting an informational meeting. Again, I found myself armed with only conventional wisdom I didn't fully agree with myself, so we decided to create a new one from scratch. A template very similar to this one was what we came up with, and it uses only forty-six words in the body of the email:

Subject: Your product management experience at Red Hat

Hi Jeff,

I'm Brooke, a fellow Duke MBA ('22). May I chat with you for a few minutes about your product management experience at Red Hat?

I am trying to learn more about product management in the North Carolina tech space, so your insights would be greatly appreciated.

Best regards,

Brooke

Brooke and I knew that any outreach email had to be short in order to get read. An email this short can be viewed entirely in a single smartphone screen without scrolling, getting to the point quickly yet respectfully—exactly what a Booster would want to see.

Furthermore, there are just not that many ways to ask for a favor. Requesting a favor from a new manager looks the same as requesting a favor from a CEO, so you don't have the work of guessing which sales points perfect strangers will find most compelling, making the email far simpler (and more authentic) to write.

In essence, the 6-Point Email is a document designed to efficiently maximize appeal to Boosters (our primary target) while inoculating against the most common reasons Boosters might not respond. In fact, each point of the 6-Point Email safeguards against a specific and common Booster concern. This first point safeguards against the scenario where a Booster wants to help but lacks the time to do so. Short emails allow for short responses; long emails do not. Let's examine this more closely.

A quick response like, "When are you available?" would be appropriate in response to a 6-Point Email. That reply can be dashed off a minute before a meeting starts or while waiting to check out at the supermarket. However, such a short, clinical reply would look rude in response to a three-hundred-word "sell yourself" email you agonized over. This effectively turns Boosters' empathy against us—because they don't have time to send a thoughtful reply, they may postpone replying *at all* until later. And all too often, later becomes never.

Although the preceding email example may be rather generic in its own right, it is still better than the alternative. Without a doubt, short and generic is far better than long and generic. It gets to the point faster—"I need a favor. Can you please help me?"—which takes less time to read and demonstrates appreciation for the recipient's busy schedule.

As a prospective hiring manager, I would imagine that this job seeker's initial outreach email is a proxy for what a project update email from them might look like—is it to the point, or does it meander before getting to the information I really want to know?

Furthermore, by keeping your initial outreach under seventy-five words, you're minimizing the chances that you'll (1) make grammatical and/or spelling mistakes or (2) accidentally alienate your Booster through your tone, word choice, or word count. More words may help you get a reluctant response from an Obligate, but we are targeting Boosters—people who genuinely enjoy helping others. Therefore, there's no need to write more—in fact, writing more just means taking on unnecessary risk. Keep it short and move on.

Okay, I understand the seventy-five word limit now, but what about the second point? Why shouldn't I mention jobs in the email?

There are two main reasons not to do this: (1) it's unnecessary (because they *already know* you're looking for a job) and (2) it's intimidating.

How do they know that if I don't tell them?

Because nobody sends emails like this for fun.

At least I hope not, because that's really messed up.

Everyone who receives an email like this knows you are looking for jobs, which is totally fine. An informational meeting request is a polite way to request a tryout with a Booster to see whether they might be willing to advocate for you within their organization.

So, if they know I'm looking for a job, isn't it fake and awkward to ask them for an informational meeting in the first place?

Of course it's awkward—it's a job search!—but it's definitely not fake. You genuinely will be seeking their advice and insight (and, later, their referrals), but most importantly, asking for an informational meeting rather than a job is just plain good manners. To bring up jobs in your first email to a potential contact is like telling a dinner party host, "I'm giving you this bottle of wine in exchange for the dinner you'll be serving me for free later this evening." There's simply no need to be that blunt.

Note that this can be confusing from a cultural perspective, particularly in the US. According to Erin Meyer's incredible book on cultural intelligence, *The Culture Map,* the US—for better and worse—is the lowest-context culture in the world, meaning we tend to say what we mean and mean what we say at nearly all times. (In general, more diverse cultures tend to be lower context simply out of necessity. When everyone shares a cultural background, much more can be communicated with a pause and body language. However, when those norms are not universally shared, communication must be much more explicit.)

However, Americans have a few exceptions to this rule. Taking gifts to parties is perhaps the best-known example of coded, high-context behavior in the US. Another exception is negative feedback; Americans tend to be painfully indirect when delivering negative feedback, creating farcical feedback sandwiches like this: "Steve, first off, we appreciate your promptness, and your penmanship is amazing, but we're going to need you to focus on getting your work done correctly and on time. That said, you're a joy to have in the office." In that formulation, a majority of the time and word count is focused on positive elements of my performance, but the intent of that mouthful was to deliver the critical feedback. By contrast, "Steve, your work is both incorrect and late" would suffice in France or Israel, for example, saving all parties a lot of time and risk of confusion.

The third big exception is job searching. Stating what is obvious— even in the US—isn't always welcome. However, some contacts prefer more explicit communications. In those cases, certainly be more direct! Being more direct is something you can quickly and visibly accomplish in response to feedback, but suddenly being more subtle isn't really a thing you can do. Thus, err on the side of subtlety, at least until you gain a sense of the predominant communication style among your potential Boosters.

Just accept that the job search has some choreography to it, and your job is to execute your steps as gracefully as possible. Being employed *anywhere* means dealing with awkward situations, and your ability to deal with this utterly predictable one is a potential Booster's best proxy for how well you would deal with awkward situations on the job.

I see why it's unnecessary, but why is mentioning jobs in the 6-Point Email intimidating?

Boosters want to help you, but their help is useful only if it's given voluntarily. One of the quickest ways to alienate a Booster is to ask for help before trying to get to know them at all. After all, in informational meetings you are hoping that contacts are willing to put their reputation on the line (ever so slightly at times, substantially at others) to vouch for you to a peer or superior in their organization.

Before Boosters are willing to do this, they must first develop a level of comfort with and trust in you. Boosters are driven by the social norms of helping people in need. However, unlike in the couch-moving experiment, Boosters do incur some risk by endorsing a candidate for a position. Thus, if you ask for their endorsement without getting to know them or giving them a chance to know you first, they may feel intimidated—as if by agreeing to conduct an informational meeting with you, they are automatically signing on to help you find a job. Therefore, they may choose not to respond at all.

Alternatively, Boosters may dismiss you directly, saying: "Sorry, I don't know anything about any current openings—good luck!" Not even Boosters want to endure the awkwardness of telling job seekers outright that they need to get to know you (and you them) better before they decide whether or not to vouch for you and pass you on, so asking about jobs in that initial email is a quick way to lose a potentially excellent contact.

Some contacts may ask you to send your resume to them right away so they can forward it on your behalf even without an informational meeting. Unfortunately, this is typically Obligate behavior—they may indeed forward your resume, which is certainly better than nothing (and may itself lead to interviews, since HR is unlikely to ask, "Are you actually recommending this person, or did you just not want to talk to them?"). Recognize that these Obligates certainly will not advocate for you, however—how could they without knowing you at all? In other words, you get what you pay for, and "earning" a Booster requires a minimal investment of time getting to know them.

What if I've already identified a job posting at their employer? Should I mention this in my outreach email?

Yes, if that's something you're comfortable with. If you have conducted the legwork and found a relevant job posting, feel free to mention it in your outreach email, as in this example:

Hi Patricia,

I'm Adrian, a fellow member of the EdTech LinkedIn Group. May I have a few minutes to ask you about your sales experience at Enspire Learning?

Your insights would be greatly appreciated, since I'm now in the process of deciding whether to apply for your open Business Development Intern position.

Best regards,

Adrian

Recall that the 6-Point Email was designed to inoculate against reasons why a Booster may not want to reply to you. One of those reasons might include anxiety about not knowing whether any open positions exist. By proactively mentioning the open position, you remove any anxiety the Booster may feel about having to do reconnaissance on your behalf.

Should I actually *apply* to that posting before I request an informational meeting?

No, not unless the posting includes an imminent deadline. I advise my students to spend at least one week trying to conduct an informational meeting prior to applying, for three important reasons.

First, a great informational meeting may make applying online unnecessary—with a Booster's support, you'd be amazed at the exceptions that can and will be made. This saves you precious job search time. I recommend not applying online to that posting until and unless the Booster advises you to do so.

Second, your informational interviewer will likely be able to give you tips about themes or experiences to stress in your application that will maximize your chance of getting noticed. (Ultimately, it'll be your contact's *referral* that gets you noticed, but asking the Booster's advice here builds that individual's willingness to make that referral. It also pays dividends during interviews: once you have an employer's attention, offering some spot-on messaging—the kind only an inside source could know—is a fast route to an offer.)

Third, you inoculate against this all-too-common scenario:

"I'd love to help. Did you find any jobs on our website?"

"Yes."

"Did you apply?"

"Yes."

"Oh, well HR will reach out if they find a match. Good luck!"

End of conversation. It's hard to come back from this. It calls into question the sincerity of your outreach, leaving your contact to wonder if you genuinely wanted their insight . . . or if you were just frustrated that you hadn't heard back from your online application. It may take a week or two to find a person, but again, the ticking time bomb scenario doesn't exist in the real world. *People don't miss out on interviews by not applying in time; people miss out on interviews by applying instead of networking.*

Why is Point #3—putting your connection first—so important?

For the same reason that nearly every pop song these days gets to its chorus within its first thirty seconds—you need to give the contact a reason to care quickly so they'll actually pay attention. Identifying your connection to the contact right up front maximizes your chance of getting your message read.

With LinkedIn Group messages, LinkedIn informs the recipient right away in the subject line that a fellow group member is messaging them, so no specific effort is necessary here.

Stating your connection to a contact is also easy when reaching out to an alum from a previous school, organization, or affinity group—simply state that connection in your first sentence, as in our first example. These contacts can be reached directly with minimal effort and typically have a high response rate, so we start with them whenever possible.

My job seekers consistently remark that writing the first "connection" sentence to a fan mail–based contact is surprisingly easy. This ease stems from the fact that there is something organic and genuine to talk about—specifically, the job seeker's interest in learning more about whatever topic the target had been interviewed about. Change the subject line around a little, and your outreach email gets even simpler to write:

Subject: Your interview in last month's *Science* magazine

Hi Dr. Johnson,

I'm just completing my biology degree at Case Western Reserve University, and I found your thoughts on the Cleveland Clinic's trial use of nanomachines to address certain forms of cancer in last month's issue of *Science* to be very interesting.

Would you mind discussing your work further with me in a brief phone chat? I had a few follow-up questions, and your insights would be invaluable.

Thank you for your time,

Caroline Thomas

Finding the article is the hard part in these outreaches (along with keeping them under seventy-five words; the excitement you feel from finding a great article can sometimes cause excessive gushiness in your word count, but be cool and maintain your form). The upside is that once that article is found, the outreach email practically writes itself.

What do I do when I don't have a connection?

Your email gets even easier! Just skip this point and embrace the fact that you are writing a complete stranger. Don't call it out. Just act as if this is completely natural, because it is. At least, it's every bit as natural as reaching out to total strangers who happened to attend the same school you did many years ago.

In other words, this is *all* totally unnatural. Lean into that fact! You will have success in your outreach from people you have absolutely no connection to, and those will become your favorite hits of all—not just because it feels like you pulled off the heist of the century, but because you know that this person is disproportionately likely to be a Booster simply *because* they responded to you despite having no connection.

In summary, in cases where you have no connection, simply skip the connection sentence and move directly to the "ask" of whether they're willing to discuss their experiences with you.

Speaking of "asks," why does the fourth point of making your request in the form of a question matter?

This is a recently added point. Those of you familiar with the first edition of this book may be wondering what happened to the 5-Point Email. Short version: In the evolution of 2HJS, the original fifth point ("Maintain control of the follow-up") has been rendered implicit and replaced by two new points, leading to its modern incarnation.

The reason Point #4 exists is to make your outreach easier and faster to respond to by directing your reader's attention to your call for action. "I was wondering if you would be able to chat with me about your product management experience at Red Hat" doesn't obviously warrant a response; "May I chat with you for a few minutes about your product management experience at Red Hat?" *does* warrant a response, since it is an actual question rather than a statement.

Question marks demand attention—namely, an answer—in a way periods do not. Plus, emails without questions take longer for a reader to register whether a response is warranted.

This directness strikes some of my job seekers as bold—who intuitively prefer wording their ask as a statement. I think this may stem from the fact that when you ask a direct question, you open yourself up to rejection in a way that you do not when you make a statement. However, it's that very risk of rejection that conveys your confidence in making the request, whereas just informing someone that you'd like to speak to them (without actually asking them to do so) suggests the opposite.

What do you mean by the fifth point—"Define your interest both narrowly and broadly"?

This advice is designed to inoculate against the scenario in which a particular Booster's own firm may not be hiring, but they may still have relevant contacts to share or helpful advice to offer. Anything is better than the "We're under a hiring freeze right now, but good luck with your search!" Booster blow-off email!

By generalizing your interest to include a logical family of similar employers that share certain traits (while still focusing your interest primarily on your target contact's employer), you accomplish two goals.

First, Boosters can be assured that your interest in their firm is sincere and logical. In our original example, Red Hat is indeed a technology company that hires product managers in North Carolina, so Brooke's outreach makes sense.

Second, it encourages Boosters at firms that aren't currently hiring to respond regardless of whether they have job opportunities internally. It's counterintuitive, but these are the best Boosters of all. I call them Super-Boosters because they can be exponentially helpful—they can help you at many employers instead of just their own. However, you only enjoy that benefit when you provide a coherent context about what you are seeking. "Marketing" or "nursing" are not specific enough—"marketing in the consumer packaged goods space" or "home care pediatric nursing" are.

To me, these several-word phrases describing your type of target employers are the modern elevator pitch—the ability to take the universe of all possible employers and narrow it to a logical subset in just a handful of words. Note that you may have several different phrases like this if you are targeting multiple spaces at once. Simply swap in the one that is relevant at the time.

That said, just because these emails are short doesn't mean they are easy to write! However, the upside is that this piece of your email is really the only place that will require customization.

If you are struggling to write a broad description of the types of firms, look back at your LAMP list and ask yourself what several or more of these employers have in common. The good news is that once you create these phrases, they will prove useful repeatedly throughout the remainder of your search to quickly establish credibility with contacts inside your desired fields. Learning the lingo is part of the challenge, and you will refine it as you talk to more and more professionals within that space. (This learning element is part of why I discourage a shotgun approach of targeting big-name employers outside of your current industry—it's hard to learn anything from one employer to the next when you're constantly changing industries, and it's also difficult to keep creating new broad definitions of your interest for 6-Point Emails in a specific enough way that will resonate with potential contacts.)

In short, if a contact tells you their employer isn't hiring but they are still happy to talk, always take that call! By remembering to define her interest broadly in addition to narrowly, Brooke offered her potential Boosters a variety of ways to help regardless of their employer's own hiring situation, turning what could have been a depressing response for all parties ("Now's not a great time at Red Hat") into a positive one ("Red Hat's not hiring right now, but if you're still interested in talking, I can tell you about what the market's like right now and point you to a few other tech firms in the area [that I know *are* hiring]"). Everyone wins.

Why does the sixth and final point, "Keep over half the word count about the *contact*, not about you," matter?

It turns out the proportion of your word count either betrays or confirms your stated intentions.

I used to allow a 6-Point Email to be up to one hundred words in length, but because the body often just takes fifty words to convey, I would see well-intentioned job seekers fill in the rest of the word count with "a little about me."

Often the word count of the "about me" dwarfed the word count about the contact. This carried a number of negative effects. It buried the request for an informational among more words, created a copy/paste feeling given that the biographical information often wasn't customized for each recipient, and—most importantly—it called into question the sincerity of the job seeker's inquiry. The words said "learn," but the word *count* said "sell!"

To avoid such a mixed message, you must show deference with your word count by keeping at least half of it devoted to the contact. The easiest way to do this is not to add more words about the contact—that can get clunky and stalker-like very quickly—but to write fewer words about yourself. Again, less is more.

How will they know who I am if I don't tell them my background?

Remember, we are relying on social norms here. The more we try to justify our request for a contact's time, the greater the risk of shifting them away from easier social norms to harder market norms.

That being said, *some* history is helpful. However, that history should not be an attached resume! I don't know about you, but I tend not to open email attachments from strangers.

In high school while first learning to drive, I came up with something I now call the *Boot Theory* that may prove instructive here, and it goes like this: don't look at anything on the side of the road while driving. If you do, it's very likely you'll see an animal who met an untimely end, and you will be sad. However, if you're lucky and you see a non-animal object on the side of the road—for example, a discarded boot (true on multiple occasions, thus the name)—you won't feel *better*. It's not a classic lose-lose situation—it's more like a lose-meh situation—but regardless, no good comes from looking at the side of the road while driving.

Opening attachments from strangers is also a lose-meh situation. Opening a job seeker's email attachment may not give you a computer virus, but it certainly won't improve your day.

The only good time to send a resume is after one is requested—never before. Sending an unrequested resume subverts the stated intent of your email (learning) and signals both desperation and a lack of social grace. If contacts want to know more about you, they will ask or look you up on LinkedIn.

However, especially if you have a common name, I do recommend having a signature file at the end of your email that lists your contact information, *including the shortcut to your LinkedIn page*, which you can customize on LinkedIn's settings page. There are nearly five thousand people named Kevin Lee on LinkedIn. Thus, if you're named Kevin Lee, the chance your contact will be able to find your profile quickly without a direct link is slim. A LinkedIn shortcut in your signature file is subtle enough that it will be spotted by those seeking more information about you but safely ignored by those who don't, ensuring you win either way.

So I've got this 6-Point Email, but you told me earlier the success rate on it is only 20 to 40 percent? Isn't there a better way to identify Boosters than emailing five to hear back from one or two?

No, sadly. However, the way each contact responds provides us with some proxy information that will allow us to approximate quickly whether a target contact is a Booster, who's likely worth our time, or an Obligate, who's likely not. That proxy information is our contact's responsiveness—more specifically, the amount of time it takes them to respond to our 6-Point Email. We cover this specific topic in chapter 7.

What if the people I reach out to have already received 6-Point Emails from other job seekers?

I get this question frequently; first off, let me say I'm flattered that you think 6-Point Emails have such mainstream potential! In practice (to date, at least), this has proved to be a nonissue, however. Those professionals I've spoken to who actually *have* recognized 6-Point Emails tend to get a kick out of spotting the wires of the magician's act, so to speak. They said it was comforting knowing that those 6-Point Email users would likely know what to do during or after the informational as well. Furthermore, even if the 6-Point Email becomes a standard taught by schools everywhere, it would still be effective simply because all possible alternatives are awful.

One awful alternative is doing nothing at all. Although this method is very popular, a 6-Point Email always outperforms no email whatsoever—guaranteed.

The second awful alternative is customizing your email to include more personalized information, like what your background is and how you think you can add value to your target employer. Sound familiar? Yes, the primary alternative to the 6-Point Email is the same old four-hundred-word "sell yourself" emails we've been sending for years. Remember? The ones that literally nobody likes? No matter how technology changes in the future, short and generic will always be preferable to long and generic. Not only does the 6-Point Email take less time to write, but it's also much easier to read, especially for your target audience of Boosters, who will ask for more background if they actually want or need it.

The third awful alternative is trying something very creative. Not only is this gimmick time-consuming to devise, but it also may repulse far more recipients than it delights (watching another person try too hard can be pretty off-putting), and Boosters don't need to be delighted in order to respond. They simply need to know you need help, so why work harder and risk alienating the very audience you're trying to attract?

In other words, there is no reason for creativity when facing a problem that already has an effective solution. The 6-Point Email is this effective solution. It is succinct, it appeals directly to your target audience's preferences, and it requires minimal thought on your part. All of these are great qualities in stressful situations. Even if 6-Point Emails gain in popularity, their use will allow hiring managers to quickly separate those candidates who are following a proactive and efficient outreach strategy from those who are not. I for one would much rather talk to candidates from the former group than those from the latter.

Finally, I personally guarantee that if too many people start using the 6-Point Email, I will address in great detail how to handle that very situation in a third edition of this book, which I will write on the newly-purchased private island I'll likely have then.

Until then? I wouldn't worry about it.

TROUBLESHOOTING

I've heard outreach emails need to be heavily customized to be successful—how do you respond to that?

Ugh. I get this question from job seekers a lot. If they don't hear the "customize emails to strangers" mantra from career coaches, they may read it on job search websites or hear it on an industry panel on this topic. The funny thing is that nobody agrees what this customization is supposed to look like.

I heard one speaker tell an audience, "If you want to get my attention for an informational meeting, you need to list your top three accomplishments in your initial outreach email"; and I heard a different speaker, with equal certainty, tell an audience that to get a response from *him*, job seekers need to think like a consultant for his organization before reaching out and propose ways they could either make or save his company money in their first outreach email. Who's right?

Who cares? Contacts who make their assistance arbitrarily difficult to earn fall firmly into the Obligate camp—they are not our target audience. There's simply no way to appeal to Obligates efficiently, since they all have arbitrary tics that you are somehow supposed to account for in advance. This is *by design*. Remember, Obligates are motivated by guilt, and the easiest way to absolve themselves of their guilt over not wanting to reciprocate networking assistance is to blame the job seeker for not

continued

approaching them "correctly" (according to whatever standards they've invented in their head).

The problem is that what works for one Obligate won't necessarily work for any other Obligate, and it will alienate all Boosters in the process. Boosters will find Obligate-oriented emails too sales-y, weird, or pushy (or all three).

Thus, whenever you receive advice about the need for customization, ask yourself if a *Booster* requires this additional level of effort. Remember the concept of *satisficing* from the introduction (see page 5)? Boosters are classic satisficers. They aren't going to judge you harshly for not being a mind reader; instead, they will empathize with your situation and want to do what they can to make your job search easier rather than harder.

So the next time a panelist, career coach, or job search columnist recommends creating and sending a PowerPoint presentation outlining a five-year plan for the role you're pursuing (or some other such nonsense) to a perfect stranger, weep briefly for those who may actually follow this advice and spend some time with a friend or loved one instead.

Should I really address my contacts by their first name?

Yes, unless you know for sure they are an MD, in which case address them as "Dr." and their last name. Other than doctors, the only people who will take offense at the use of their first names are Obligates, and again, they're not our target audience!

The problem with honorifics like Mr., Mrs., and Ms. is that they are gender- (and marital status-) specific, and you won't know either piece of information in advance. Even if you did, I'd still opt for first names. It portrays confidence and casualness, whereas formal use of honorifics can often come across as awkwardly formal or obsequious.

TROUBLESHOOTING

Should I suggest times I'm available to speak in my 6-Point Emails?

No! There are several downsides to doing so. The first downside is that it takes time—so, so much time—to pick through your calendar and stitch together a number of possible options for a contact to claim. Some may involve moving your lunch break or missing part of a meeting or other inconveniences, so this simple act of proposing times can involve incurring a lot of additional stress.

The second downside is that calendars change. A time that may have been available two days ago may no longer be available—it may even have been claimed by a different job search contact from your Top 5—so you need to either (1) suggest unique times to each specific contact (to avoid the chance of double-booking), (2) move or cancel conflicting appointments (if that's even possible), or (3) risk looking like a flake to your brand-new contact by saying the time you offered is actually no longer available. All bad options.

The third downside is that the people you are emailing may be Curmudgeons who never respond or Obligates who don't want to respond, so you exerted a bunch of effort performing calendar surgery for someone who has no interest in helping you.

None of these are good outcomes, and all are the direct result of doing more work! That's not a good average rate of return on effort, right?

Instead, save proposing times for when you get an initial response from a contact. True, some of these will be Obligates who will stop responding once you offer specific times, but you will at least avoid pouring a bunch of time into suggesting times to Curmudgeons who totally ignore you, and that itself is a win. Rest assured that anyone who does not respond *because* you didn't include times in your original outreach email is an Obligate by definition, and therefore they are not our target audience. You will save a lot of time, effort, and stress by waiting until your second

continued

email exchange with a new contact to start aligning calendars, I assure you!

I tend to perform better in person than by phone— can I request an in-person informational? If so, when should I do this?

My recommendation is, once your contact has responded positively to your initial 6-Point Email, state that you would be happy to chat in person or by phone. (If you are so inclined, mention Skype as an option as well.) Your contact can opt in to whichever format they prefer. It is important to recognize that while *you* may prefer meeting in person, many of your contacts will not.

However, do not feel obligated to offer an in-person option if you are not locally based. If you still want to, try to organize informationals in your targeted city into a single week. This will keep the costs manageable, show your commitment to relocating, and demonstrate that you have already built up simultaneous interest at other organizations.

Many of the contacts I found are less experienced than I am. Is the 6-Point Email designed for younger job seekers more so than older ones?

Yes and no. Yes, the examples provided here work best when approaching contacts who are equally or more experienced than you are. However, the same general rules of the 6-Point Email apply when approaching less experienced contacts for assistance.

Remember that your contact has no incentive to help you other than altruism. Thus, Boosters will *always* be your target, because they are the segment most likely to willingly incur inconvenience to help someone in need. In other words, you need them to like you enough to want to assist.

A common mistake I see experienced job seekers make is trying to impress younger contacts with their relevant experience—this is rather wrong-headed. The informational interview is about the contact, not the job seeker (unless the contact wants it to be)—that personal connection, not their assessment of your qualifications, is what earns their advocacy.

The only minor changes to the outreach format will be an emphasis on learning more about the contact's experience rather than their insights. You'll still be asking the person for advice during the informational interview itself; however, it will be more of the "How can I best navigate your organization?" variety than the "What should I do in my first thirty days to get off to a fast start?" kind. The resulting outreach email will look something like this:

Subject: Your finance experience at Reebok

Hi Anjali,

My name is Terry Ray, and I've enjoyed your comments in LinkedIn's Sports Apparel Group. May I have a few minutes to ask you about your finance experience with Reebok?

Your insights would be deeply appreciated, since I am now seeking to return to Boston to be closer to family after spending the last few years in corporate finance at Nike.

Best regards,

Terry

continued

TROUBLESHOOTING

This email still shows deference to the contact's expertise in his employer's inner workings without taking a deferential approach that may create awkwardness when approaching a junior colleague. However, it is important to recognize that Boosters come in all ages, levels of authority, and functions throughout organizations, so it indeed pays to take a genuine interest in the stories of everyone you approach in this process. In addition, younger people in most cultures still tend to reflexively defer to older people—in professional settings in particular. Therefore, a junior contact may be even more likely to advocate for you than someone similar to you in age simply because it's common courtesy.

TRACK

I *know* I'm supposed to track my outreach, so can I skip this chapter?

Unfortunately, most job seekers I work with know they are supposed to track their outreach, but they do so either poorly or not at all. Either way, it's devastating to a job search, and it is shockingly common. Thus the purpose of this chapter is to provide you with a simple yet effective method—which I call the 3B7 Routine—for systematically managing the outreach you initiate.

The most common version of tracking outreach poorly is using a spreadsheet (LAMP list or otherwise). Job seekers who go down this path hate life every time they look at that Excel file, because spreadsheets are reactive rather than proactive; they are better at highlighting what you forgot to do yesterday rather than what you need to do today.

This is because *a spreadsheet is not a calendaring tool*! It has no alarms or action prompts, yet I'm shocked by how many people try to use it as such. Microsoft Outlook or Google Calendar *do* have calendar functionality, but job seekers for whatever reason seem to prefer "having all their work in one place" (a common Defensive Job Search preference, as outlined on page 6) to effectively tracking their outreach. Resist the urge!

You said I'm only targeting five employers right now, though—can't my memory handle that?

Perhaps, but you're thinking clearly now. Remember temporal construal theory from chapter 1? That concept says we make better decisions in advance than we do in the heat of the moment. Your memory is behaving very rationally right now, focusing on how important it is to you to start lining up interviews. However, when it comes time to follow up on an unresponsive contact—a task you may consider awkward or unsavory (less important considerations than securing new employment)—you tend to prioritize fleeting distractions over more serious ones.

Furthermore, your brain has been neurochemically compromised.

Wait, what?

Job searches are stressful. Stress causes the brain to produce cortisol (a stress hormone). One unfortunate side effect of cortisol is memory loss. Thus, the more stressed out you get, the more forgetful you become. Furthermore, it doesn't matter where this stress originates! It can be work-related, home-related, or personal life–related, yet it still yields the same result.

Also, job searches take time and effort, which leads to exhaustion. Many job seekers choose to combat this exhaustion with caffeine, but, sadly, caffeine consumption *also* produces cortisol in the brain. (Brains just can't catch a break.) Left unchecked, overindulgence in a cocktail of stress, exhaustion, and caffeine can send job seekers into a cortisol-fueled death spiral.

So, between temporal construal theory and cortisol, I'm going to go ahead and bet on your memory *not* being able to handle the amount of outreach that lies ahead of you! I hope you agree. Thus, a tracking system is necessary if you want all the great work you've put in so far to pay off effectively.

So, will any tracking system do?

No, not if efficiency is your goal. Although any tracking system is better than no tracking system, the tracking system I'm about to teach you (the 3B7 Routine) was designed specifically to work seamlessly in tandem with the 6-Point Emails you learned to write in chapter 6.

In the 3B7 Routine, you'll be letting a computer (specifically, your email software program's calendar) do all of your remembering for you, sending you pop-up notices whenever it is time to act. This allows you to blissfully forget about the dozens of job search tasks you'll do over the next few weeks and focus instead on just the one or two things that you must do today. Better yet, it manages all of this without your having to remember a single thing or even look at your LAMP list.

Your LAMP list remains purely a strategy document, *not* a tracking document. You refer to LAMP only when you have time to initiate outreach to a new employer (and thus need to see who's next on your list) or when you want to add new employers to it. However, it'll be at least a week before you need to do either of those things, so feel free to close your LAMP list for now.

The 3B7 Routine works so well in the 2HJS context because it helps you quickly estimate the customer segment (Curmudgeons, Obligates, or Boosters) of each person you email. It gives you a set of precise rules for your follow-up efforts—specifically when to follow up, how to do so, and when to move on—depending on the customer segment you appear to have contacted.

What exactly is the 3B7 Routine, then?

First off, it is an email tracking *routine*, or algorithm. It is standard and replicable—there is no thought, no decision making, and no decision anxiety involved, just simple execution.

The "B" in 3B7 stands for "business days"—your contacts are unlikely to be at work on weekends, so we put our job search efforts on the same schedule. (Plus, you need a couple of days off per week from your job search as well!) The "3" and the "7" refer to the number of business days before we receive a reminder to take further action, if necessary.

Our three-business-days-later (3B) reminder notifies us whether the contact we reached out to is likely to be a Booster. As I joked earlier, there is no checkbox in LinkedIn where people indicate whether they're Boosters or Curmudgeons! Therefore, we must find proxy information we can use to approximate which contact segment they belong to. Response time is that proxy.

If contacts *ever* respond to our outreach, we can assume (by definition) that they are not Curmudgeons since Curmudgeons simply never write back under any circumstances. Therefore, the only people we get responses back from are either Obligates or Boosters. Thankfully, those two groups respond differently.

Boosters empathize with the difficulties of being in a job search, so they will do their best to get back to you promptly. Obligates tend to drag their feet before replying, since they don't genuinely want to do so in the first place.

Having overseen many job searches, I've found that a majority of employer contacts whom I would define as Boosters respond within 3B, or three business days. Look at it this way—if you make a time-sensitive request, would someone who is genuinely interested in your welfare habitually wait a week to respond to you?

This rule of thumb is by no means perfect, but using the 80/20 Rule, we can assume that contacts who get back to us within 3B are likely to be Boosters and we can hold off on contacting anyone else. At least that will be our working assumption until they give us reason to believe otherwise.

If we do not hear back from a contact within 3B of sending our email, we'll assume the recipient is either an Obligate (who tends to delay responding) or a Curmudgeon (who will never respond), and move on.

It is too soon to follow up, however! Following up after just 3B is by far the most common mistake made by aspiring 3B7 users. However, we're also fairly certain at this point we won't hear back, so what can we do? We'll initiate outreach to a second contact *at the same employer* to see whether that person might be a Booster instead. Yes, these emails will be very similar, and if the two contacts were to share your emails with one another, they might notice some similarities! That's why we wait 3B before sending an additional 6-Point Email to someone else in that organization. Furthermore, unless the email is a disaster or distributed in abnormally high volume—more about this shortly—sharing informational meeting requests with colleagues for scrutiny is not a thing people actually do! And if our second contact doesn't respond, three business days later, we'll try a third contact, and so on. This allows us to hedge our bets and maintain progress, given that it is unlikely—not impossible, but unlikely—that our first contact will respond if they haven't already done so.

Our second reminder, which is set for seven business days (7B) after our initial outreach email, is the one that triggers a follow-up. It has been a week and a half, since our initial attempt, which to me is just right for following up (in the US, at least—see the "Troubleshooting" section for more information on this). One week can be seen as too abrupt, but two weeks suggests a lack of urgency; both are undesirable impressions to leave.

So how do I actually use the 3B7 Routine?

It's surprisingly simple—anytime you send an email to a new contact, you set two reminders in your calendar: one for 3B and one for 7B. For example, if we send an email to our favorite starter contact at BiffCo (let's call him Ed) on Monday, March 2, we will set our 3B reminder for Thursday, March 5, and our 7B reminder for Wednesday, March 11 (seven business days after the original email was sent, but nine calendar days later).

Often the most efficient way to set calendar reminders is to just create an appointment for the first thing in the morning. That way, when you first check your computer that morning, a pop-up box should be waiting on the computer's desktop and you have all day to take the necessary action signified by that reminder—either emailing a new contact if it is a 3B reminder or following up on a previous contact if it is a 7B reminder.

In your calendar, this process will look like this:

MON	TUE	WED	THU	FRI
2	3	4	5	6
Today: Send Ed Biffco 6-Point Email			7AM: 3B Ed BiffCo	
9	10	11	12	13
		7AM: 7B Ed BiffCo		

So, what do I do with these reminders?

Your actions will differ according to how your contacts respond. We address our best-case scenario first.

SCENARIO #1: FIRST CONTACT RESPONDS WITHIN THREE BUSINESS DAYS

If your initial contact (Ed) responds to you before your 3B reminder pops up on March 5 (within three business days), then congratulations! This is both the best-case and the easiest-to-track scenario. Ed appears to be a Booster, so set up an informational meeting with him for a later date—something that fits his schedule if he offers you specific times and dates in his reply—and cancel your follow-up reminders. (Don't worry about how to actually conduct those informational meetings just yet—we cover that in chapter 8.) If Ed does not offer specific times, reply with a simple email that offers a variety of times you could speak in the next week to discuss, like this:

Subject: RE: Your project management experience at BiffCo

Hi Ed,

Thank you for your quick response and willingness to chat. Over the next week, I am free after 1pm on both Monday and Tuesday as well as all day on Wednesday—will any of those times work for you?

Thank you again,

Steve

You can reduce their own decision anxiety by giving them several options (as in the example above). These Boosters are people too, and too many options can paralyze them as well.

However, if our 3B reminder pops up and we *haven't* gotten a response from our initial contact, it appears they are a Curmudgeon or Obligate and thus unlikely to respond, so we'll want to hedge our bets and move on to Scenario #2.

SCENARIO #2: FIRST CONTACT DOES NOT RESPOND WITHIN THREE BUSINESS DAYS

As I mentioned earlier, in general I see a 20 to 40 percent response rate with 6-Point Emails—thus, a majority of the time you will not hear back within 3B. What do you do then?

Well, if you're like most untrained job seekers, you wait. And wait. And wait some more.

This is a *very* dangerous time for unsophisticated job seekers—specifically, ones who view contacts as a homogeneous, interchangeable bunch rather than as a grab-bag assortment of Curmudgeons, Obligates, and Boosters. They so greatly fear offending anyone that they'll postpone following up on any unanswered outreach as long as possible—often forever.

Unfortunately, they won't just own up to the fact. They'll debate that decision one anxious night after another ("Should I follow up today? That'll be so awkward! Plus, I have this big meeting to prepare for tomorrow. I'll for sure follow up tomorrow, maybe . . .") until they finally move on.

Without a formal process in place before starting, it will *always* seem safer to give contacts one more day to respond than to reach out to them a second time, acknowledging the awkward fact that they didn't respond to your first message. Unsurprisingly, in the heat of the moment most job seekers choose the comfortable path of delaying follow-up (just as temporal construal theory would predict!) despite the ineffectiveness of this approach and the decision anxiety and self-loathing it causes.

Thankfully, 2HJS users have prepared in advance for this precise scenario, choosing their follow-up routine based on when the email was *sent* rather than after it has been ignored, so they know exactly what to do—quickly draft and send a very similar 6-Point Email to their second-favorite contact.

Because this email will be your first outreach to your second contact, you will once again follow the 3B7 Routine and set 3B and 7B reminders on that person as well.

Returning to our calendar example for our first BiffCo contact, we now want to add reminders for our second contact (let's call her Ana) at BiffCo because our first contact appears not to be a Booster. Our calendar now looks like this (with our previous reminders now listed in italics):

MON	TUE	WED	THU	FRI
2	3	4	5	6
Send 6-Point Email to Ed BiffCo			Today: Send 6-Point Email to Ana BiffCo *3B Ed BiffCo*	
9	10	11	12	13
	7AM: 3B Ana BiffCo	*7B Ed BiffCo*		
16	17	18	19	20
7AM: 7B Ana BiffCo				

IN MY OUTREACH EMAIL TO CONTACT #2, SHOULD I MENTION THAT I ALREADY CONTACTED SOMEONE ELSE?

No. It may appear as if you are "tattling" on contact #1 (Ed in our BiffCo example) and that is not the sort of first impression you want to give. Simply write the same 6-Point Email to contact #2 (Ana), making no mention to Ana that she was your second choice.

STILL, WON'T THE INITIAL CONTACT BE OFFENDED THAT I CONTACTED SOMEONE ELSE?

No. In fact, you'll be doing them a favor.

Curmudgeons *certainly* don't mind if you reach out to someone else, because they are never going to write you back anyway. Obligates might weakly pretend to mind, but they will actually be relieved that someone else who cares more about your welfare has stepped in, relieving them of their Obligate guilt.

Boosters are the only audience that could possibly mind. However, if you've given them a few days to respond and then reach out to one more person, your additional effort reflects positively rather than negatively on you.

If you've heard horror stories about employers rejecting candidates who contacted multiple employees at one time, it is because the candidate contacted many (five or more) people simultaneously, requesting informational meetings. (I don't want to generalize because generalizing is bad, but it's always investment bankers who do this. Always.) Not only is this a bad use of the job seeker's time (too many similar conversations at one employer), but it also demonstrates a lack of respect for that firm's need for actual productivity from its employees.

The crucial difference between the 3B7 Routine and the horror story is that the former uses a serial process appropriately, whereas the latter uses a parallel process inappropriately.

What are serial and parallel processes?

A *serial process* is a linear sequence of events. Imagine going through the drive-through at a fast-food restaurant where there are multiple stops. At the first stop, the giant menu with the intercom, you place your order. Then you pull forward to the second stop, where you pay. Then you pull up to the final stop, where you pick up your food, and finally you drive away. This is a serial process—one step at a time.

Serial processes are good at controlling volume—for example, the fast-food restaurant has a limited number of cooks, so the number of orders they can handle per hour is also limited. Therefore, it would be a bad idea to open more stations where customers could place an order, because the cooks are the bottleneck (another name for the slowest step in a given process, which in turn determines that process's top achievable speed), resulting in even longer wait times for those who have (more quickly) placed orders.

A *parallel process* is one in which certain steps are done simultaneously. Think of going to the supermarket and seeing many lanes open through which you can check out—that is a parallel process. If the supermarket is very busy, the store may move personnel away from stocking shelves to operate the checkout lanes, reducing the amount of time people must wait before they can purchase their goods and return home.

Parallel processes are good at being fast and flexible. If a certain step in a process is slow, devoting more people to that step will speed up the entire process. In this job search process, the slow step is waiting for people to get back to you, but that doesn't mean emailing many people at once is an effective way to speed it up.

The horror story situation I mentioned earlier is sadly a true one. A former student of mine emailed nearly ten bankers at his top-choice firm simultaneously (in parallel) to request informational meetings, thinking that would help him jump-start his banking search. However, these bankers sat right next to each other, so they quickly realized they had been spammed by a job seeker, and this student's overzealous outreach quickly became the subject of ridicule.

A parallel process is indeed the fastest way for this student to find a contact. It would always be the correct approach if none of the contacts could communicate with each other and the student had an infinite amount of time to conduct informational meetings with anyone who said yes. Unfortunately, just like the Disney song says, "It's a small world, after all," and none of us have infinite time.

A serial process, although slower, is more appropriate for job search outreach—at least initially. The 3B7 Routine actually represents a serial/parallel hybrid: you start with one contact at a time (serially), but if they don't get back to you within three business days, you reach out to a second contact in parallel. This doubles your chance of finding a Booster at a target employer quickly without risking alienation from the organization along the way. (And of course you'll be reaching out to five employers in parallel at one time as well.)

Ideally, the first Booster you find at the firm will be able to play traffic cop and point you to the best person to talk to next, helping you find the hiring manager in just one additional informational meeting instead of two or more. Thus, not only does a serial/parallel hybrid demonstrate project professionalism, it also saves you time.

Back to the BiffCo example: What if I don't hear from the second contact either?

You move on to a third contact, then a fourth, and so on.

Should I reach out to a third contact even before I follow up with my first contact?

Yes! You got it! Just shut off your brain when you start this process. Follow the 3B7 rules exactly, and you'll see both just how simple 3B7 is and how scalable it is as well, easily accommodating additional contacts and even employers (though this happens a bit later) in your existing process with minimal additional effort.

When do I give up on an employer?

Only when (1) you run out of people, which really only happens at start-ups and very small employers; or (2) you are so frustrated by getting ignored by people at this organization that your motivation to pursue them actually drops, knocking them out of your Top 5.

Both of these situations are rare, though!

Okay, when my 7B reminder pops up, how do I follow up with people who haven't responded?

In the original version of this book, I recommended following up by phone, but business norms have changed in the last few years.

Now, everyone (self included) seems to hate the phone, so following up by email is totally acceptable and, in many cases, preferred by both parties. Plus, it means not having to try to track down phone numbers or navigate corporate voicemail prompts.

So, what exactly do I say in this email?

There are two schools of thought here. I typically hate providing multiple schools of thought because it causes decision anxiety, but each has its own pros and cons, so I'll let you decide for yourself.

The first school of thought (my original one) is to Reply All to your previous message and write something like this:

Subject: RE: Your project management experience at BiffCo

Hi Ed,

I just wanted to follow up on my message from last week. Might this week be a more convenient time for you to chat about your BiffCo experience? Please let me know if so!

Best regards,

Steve

The second school of thought was the brainchild of my former Fuqua career center colleague Malcom. Malcom's nickname is "Cool Breeze" for his easy-going nature, and his follow-up approach very much reflects this. He simply pretends the first email never existed and sends the exact same email seven business days later. His primary motivation is to avoid embarrassing the contact, so he doesn't call attention to the fact this is a second attempt.

The major advantage of Malcom's approach is that it minimizes complexity—literally, there is no editing required on your message before you send it a second time, saving you time and effort.

However, Malcom and I have very different primary motivations with our 7B follow-up emails. Whereas Malcom wants to minimize awkwardness, I want to avoid fundamental attribution error.

What is fundamental attribution error?

Fundamental attribution error is a behavioral psychology concept that states people tend to internalize successes and externalize failures. Put another way, if your team does well on a project, you tend to attribute it to the hard work and ideas you yourself contributed; however, if your team does poorly, you tend to attribute it to the faults and short-comings of your colleagues. (I know this isn't flattering information, but it's just human nature so please don't beat yourself up about it,)

In our situation, if you as a job seeker reach out once and never follow up (or your follow-up email is not known to be a second attempt), it's easy for an Obligate to blame you—the person they are ignoring—for the missed connection. "Any responsible job seeker would have followed up with me if this was a job they truly wanted!"

Keep in mind that—by dint of our selecting functionally relevant contacts for outreach and starting with our Top 5 employers—some of these Obligates and Boosters who initially ignore you may end up interviewing you later, since these are your dream employers, and you will keep approaching people until you find a genuine Booster who will help you get an interview. Thus, if we can't enlist them as advocates *for* us, we at least want to inoculate against them advocating *against* us. One, and only one, follow-up attempt serves that purpose, removing their ability to blame us for their lack of a response and in doing so (perhaps begrudgingly) acquiring their tacit, guilt-driven support.

That follow-up attempt may also garner a response from a contact as well, either from a Booster who had been very busy the prior week or from an Obligate who—while they may have been able to plead "missed your email" ignorance after your first attempt—can't rationalize ignoring you a second time when you followed up responsibly in an appropriate amount of time. Either way, more traction is better than less. Despite the fact that Obligates are not our target audience, they can still provide valuable assistance (despite themselves).

Which approach should I choose???

Yeah, sorry about that. Decision anxiety is not awesome.

Short answer: Use whichever approach makes it easier for you to send your 7B follow-up *with 100 percent certainty*. I can't stress this enough—the 3B7 Routine is baking, not cooking!

Cooking is an imprecise, almost romantic pastime, where approximation rather than exact measurement is expected and anything can be corrected with salt and pepper in the end. It is the 80/20 Rule brought to life! Those who enjoy cooking are like swashbucklers in the kitchen, improvising as they go and fully confident that their outcomes will at least be serviceable if not transcendent.

Baking, however, is an *excruciatingly* precise activity. There is no correcting with salt and pepper later. If you add the wrong amount of salt, or add it at the wrong time, your cake simply won't rise and you'll have to start over again. It is unforgiving—more a science than an art, as cooking is.

Much of 2HJS is like cooking, where being imprecise is perfectly okay—advantageous, even. However, 3B7 (and tracking, more generally) is one of the few spots where 2HJS more resembles baking than cooking. The steps must be executed *exactly*—like clockwork—in order to derive any benefit from them, let alone to keep your outreach process sustainable as your volume ramps up.

The key is just to be sure you send a follow-up—*any* follow-up—after seven business days. It gives you a definitive way to shut the book on this contact if they choose not to respond at this point, and it gives you a second chance at getting a relevant contact's attention.

Personally, I would blend the best of both worlds. I'd send the exact same message (Malcolm's approach) but through a different channel, using the next method down the list on page 92.

This would all be easier with a visual— can you lay out 3B7 in a diagram?

Will this do?

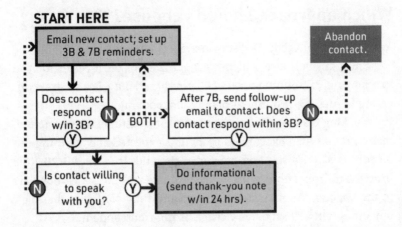

Yes, thank you. Shouldn't I follow up with a contact more than just one time, though?

I don't recommend it. The people who would respond after a third attempt would typically be Obligates rather than Boosters, and because they generally offer a negative return on investment, it's best to take their not-so-subtle hint and move on after your one follow-up attempt.

So, what if I hear back from my second contact within three business days *and* my first contact after I send them a 7B follow-up?

You do two informationals! There's nothing wrong with networking with two people at the same firm simultaneously. We just want to limit the occasions where we do this, if possible. Perhaps one or the other of the contacts who responds proves to be an Obligate who gets very vague when you ask for guidance on how to proceed, so having a backup isn't a bad thing. However, seeking backups in all cases, even when our first contact seems to be uber-engaged, is not efficient.

One Candidate, Two Outcomes

I met Shaun after one of my talks. His story is just too perfect not to share in this book.

Shaun wanted to work for a major consulting firm that did not visit his campus to recruit. He applied online but did not hear anything back for several weeks. So he decided to give 2HJS a try and started reaching out to consultants at the company to ask them for informational meetings. After a few conversations, he got a referral to HR. This led to three rounds of interviews. Finally, after a month or two of networking effort, Shaun's dream came true—he got an offer with his top-choice employer.

The story doesn't end there, though . . . .

The very next day, Shaun received an email from the employer. Figuring it was his offer letter, he opened the email and read, "Dear Shaun, Thank you for your application. The talent pool was very competitive this year, however, and we are unable to offer you an interview at this time. . . ."

No, Shaun's offer wasn't rescinded. He simply received the automatically generated email from the consulting firm's online application system letting him know that their "database didn't detect a match."

The same exact candidate received two very different outcomes based on the way he approached the firm. In fact, as far as the firm's IT system was concerned, Shaun was two completely different people!

So the next time you feel obligated to apply before you start networking, remember that they are two entirely different processes.

What if a contact responds to me very late? Like a month or more later?

In this case, assuming you have found better options in the interim, thank your long-delayed contact for their response, update them on your progress, and wish them a nice day. You have no reason to feel bad in this case—just as nobody would feel bad moving on from a plumber or mechanic who waited weeks to return a call. No job seeker should rely on contacts who behave similarly.

Okay, so I understand the 3B7 Routine for BiffCo. What do I do with my other Top 5 target employers?

The exact same thing! Although I advocate using a (primarily) serial process for each particular employer, I advocate using a parallel process across several employers. Thus, you'll be conducting the 3B7 Routine for multiple employers simultaneously.

How many employers should I contact at one time?

Only five, at least to start with—that's what the ten-minute duration specified at the start of this chapter assumes. Because the typical hit rate on 6-Point Emails is about 20 to 40 percent, that means you should hear back from one or two of the first five contacts you reach out to (one at each of your Top 5 target employers in your LAMP list) within three business days. This allows you to get an informational or two scheduled and under way while you wait to branch out and follow up with the others.

What if I need a job, like, *now*? Can I start with more than five employees or employers?

You can, but I wouldn't. I've literally never seen anyone successfully use 3B7 starting with more than five employers in their initial outreach. Not only is tracking more than five employers more challenging when you're still learning the process, but it also puts you at risk of getting overwhelmed by your initial response.

It's not unheard of to get a 100 percent response rate on your first batch of emails! I frequently hear from job seekers who go five for five. It makes for a busy first week of rapidly scheduling informationals, but it is doable. However, scheduling seven or eight informationals in your first week of using 3B7, especially on top of other school, professional, or personal obligations, is not really feasible, given most of your informationals are done during business hours.

In essence, the 3B7 Routine starts your outreach off on training wheels—it will feel like there is so much more you could be doing, but, to borrow a phrase from the military, "slow is smooth, and smooth is fast." In other words, when you try to rush ahead, your technique becomes sloppy and your (inevitable) mistakes cost you far more time than your haste has saved.

Slow is *smart* when embracing a new way of doing things. You are assuming an executive role in your job search as opposed to the worker-bee role you may have been accustomed to in your prior searches. This is a massive adjustment at first, given how ingrained the Defensive Job Search mind-set of quantifying progress in hours worked and applications submitted is, but starting slow and smooth results in far greater results from your effort!

Think of this process less as a lot of disjointed emails and more as a strategic email campaign. In a campaign, many disparate elements (emails in this case) work together in tandem rather than isolation. In 3B7, every email serves a purpose, just as every pause between emails does. If you learn the basics well, you won't even notice as the complexity of what you are accomplishing ramps up.

Okay, so I'll start with five—when can I add more employers?

The earliest I'd recommend adding a sixth or seventh simultaneous employer to your outreach is after you've completed three rounds of 3B7 (meaning you've reached out to your third contacts at thus far unresponsive employers) with flawless tracking and you feel you have the hang of it. It's a pretty simple process once you get into it. You'll see quickly there is an economy of scale once you've established the proper habit of setting 3B and 7B reminders whenever you email someone for the first time.

That said, perfect execution is far more important than volume—try to do too much right away and you risk spreading yourself too thin. Sadly, a slow response to a Booster who offers times for an informational is one of the two quickest ways to lose that Booster. (We'll address the second way in chapter 10.)

TROUBLESHOOTING

What if I get an out-of-office reply to my 6-Point Email?

Simply move back your 3B and 7B reminders on that contact by the corresponding number of business days. Yes, they might be inundated by work email when they return to the office after a vacation or business trip, but Boosters are Boosters at the end of the day—they generally make it happen.

That said, if they are going to be out of the office for more than three business days from when you wrote, try a new contact immediately so you don't lose an entire business week waiting for someone who may or may not reply.

TROUBLESHOOTING

Do I really need to follow up with contact #1 if I get no response, even if contact #2 does respond?

Yes, absolutely. You are the one that serves to benefit most from these informational meetings, so the onus of effort to make them happen is on you. The follow-up email not only gives you a second chance to get the help of a busy Booster (or susceptible Obligate), but also gives you a clear-cut "backstop" of effort for that contact—meaning, if they don't respond then, we can safely move on and forget that person ever existed.

Just kidding.

Slightly.

Without a plan in place, the sheer quantity of rejections and getting ignored in this process will drive you mad. People simply don't have many venues in life where they must come to terms with efforts that only work out 20 to 40 percent of the time. Can you think of any?

Thus, I recommend not even thinking of these people as *people* when you email them; instead, consider them lottery tickets with 20 to 40 percent odds of success. After you email them, don't think about them again until either (1) they respond to you within 3B, in which case they are saints and scholars and you will honor them or (2) your 7B reminder pops up and you have to remember what name to address your follow-up email to. That's it. Don't dwell on the failures because there will be a lot of them. Focus on the successes. After all, it's the very scarcity of Boosters themselves that makes 2HJS so effective—if *everyone* was a Booster, your soon-to-be-realized competitive advantage from targeting them exclusively would disappear.

Furthermore, since no step in this process is optional—meaning you *will* follow up with unresponsive contacts—you actually save both time and anxiety. It's far quicker to mindlessly crank out an obligatory follow-up email than it

continued

is to debate whether or not doing so is worth your time (again, temporal construal theory in action).

In short, optional activities are harder to be motivated for than mandatory ones. Think of following up on unresponsive contacts as the equivalent of going to the dentist—it's not for you to like; it's for you to do.

So when do I actually apply online to jobs?

The conventional wisdom is "apply as soon as possible," but this is short-sighted guidance. Sure, online job postings cost no money to apply to, but applying to them is not a free activity; it costs you time, effort, and confidence. Thus, I disagree with anyone who says applying online "can't hurt"—it hurts you every time you do it, and those who say otherwise simply think very little of your time, effort, and sanity.

On the other hand, I do think there are a couple of less bad (i.e., better) times to apply for jobs. The first is just before a stated deadline; not many jobs post hard deadlines like that, especially outside of campus interview infrastructures. (Government roles are the ones who most commonly feature hard and unforgiving deadlines, but thankfully these deadlines are typically publicly posted.) The second is after a week of unsuccessful outreach, meaning you've tried two relevant contacts (three business days apart, following 3B7) and have yet to get an engaged response from a potential Booster.

In your outreach step, the bottleneck is waiting for people to get back to you. Thus days where you're between 3B and 7B reminders, waiting for people to get back to you is a great time to put forth your perfunctory online job applications.

That being said, taking breaks is also a critical part of this process—3B7 works because it is *finite.* At a certain point, you've done all you can and you need the engagement of others to proceed further. Thus, if you wake up one day and see no 3B or 7B reminders on your computer's desktop,

TROUBLESHOOTING

take the day off! Go see a movie, grab dinner with loved ones, hit the bars early—whatever you're into, do that! It's when the job search seems never-ending that job seekers succumb to the Impostor Syndrome we mentioned in the introduction—as in, "I should be doing *more*!"

Rest assured, if you are executing 3B7 precisely for your Top 5 without exception, you are doing everything that could reasonably be expected of you. Let me repeat this. *You are doing everything that could reasonably be expected of you.*

You are doing executive-level work in this job search and that means spending more time thinking and less time doing—all in the name of achieving far greater impact. It takes nerve and confidence to embrace this executive role. Negative, doubting thoughts will assail you, berating you for "not doing more," but that is the Defensive Job Search's last gasp to try to win you back to the dark side.

I assure you that you, like tens of thousands of people before you, are doing the right thing by giving this process a chance. For right now, just do your best to forgive yourself for any paranoia you might be feeling—it's completely natural, and that self-doubt will dissipate quickly once your informational meetings start in the next few days!

Part 2: Contact Wrap-Up

Launching Part 2: Contact with a plan in place is critical, because getting back to potential Boosters within twenty-four hours is absolutely essential. Setting 3B and 7B reminders each time you send an email may feel odd, especially given that the person may write you right back within minutes. However, *it frees up your mind to focus on those who reward your attention*—a much healthier perspective to keep throughout this process.

I often see my students fall weeks behind on sending thank-you emails to the contacts they've spoken to—they simply become busy, and then they'll ask me, "Is three days/three weeks/three months too long to wait to send a thank-you email?"

Thank-you notes are electronic receipts that you spoke to someone. I have an awful memory, so at my previous jobs I had an email folder called "Thank yous" where I'd file any thank-you note I got to help me remember any job seeker I spoke to, knowing that my memory inevitably would fail me. We further explore how to write and follow up on these thank-you emails in chapter 10, but I want to make a broader point here before continuing.

All the hard work you put in during the outreach process can be squandered very quickly if you don't respond appropriately to the people who are trying to help you. Don't fixate on those who haven't responded yet; let your 3B and 7B reminders guide you through managing those frustrating contacts while you spend your time focusing on those who are most likely to help you find jobs.

PART 3

Convince: Informational Meetings

RESEARCH

I know I'm supposed to research employers, but how much research is enough?

Research is like learning or practicing—there's no explicit finish line, which indeed makes advice like "research employers" rather maddening to receive. The purpose of this chapter isn't to teach you how to research for term papers, investments, or even actual job interviews (though it will have some parallels to that last one).

No, the purpose of this chapter is to teach you how to research for informational meetings. There is a lot that *could* be researched for informationals but only a few key items that absolutely *must* be—separating the wheat from the chaff first involves understanding what informational meetings are.

So, what exactly *is* an informational meeting?

An informational meeting is a conversation between an information seeker (usually a job hunter, but not always) and an information keeper (usually an employee at a job seeker's target employer, but not always).

The information seeker leads the conversation to collect relevant information about the information keeper's career with the target employer.

This was first coined back in 1970 by Richard Bolles in *What Color Is Your Parachute?*, and it still hasn't gone out of style. In fact, it is more important now than ever before, because these days no hiring manager has time to genuinely consider every resume or CV that gets submitted to each online job posting. That said, the act of conducting an informational meeting used to itself be sufficient for advancing you in the process. Today, informationals must be effectively parlayed in order to land an actual job interview, so we'll roughly break down Part 3 as follows:

CHAPTER #	ESTIMATED TIME REQUIRED
Chapter 8: Research	~15 minutes
Chapter 9: Discuss	~30 minutes
Chapter 10: Follow-Up	Ongoing
Total for Part 3: Convince	~45 minutes per informational

The goal of an informational meeting is twofold: first, to build rapport, and second, to gain usable information. Of the two, the first is more important, because if rapport is established, then usable information can be collected at a later date. The same cannot be said about prioritizing useful information over connecting with your interviewer.

Why should I bother with informationals when I can just apply online directly?

If the job search were logical and fair, job postings would absolutely be a more direct route to employment than roundabout informational meetings. However, remember that the job search is not fair in the traditional sense, where whoever has the best qualifications wins— it's fair in the modern sense, where job seekers have metaphorically all been given a brand-new board game and whoever figures it out *fastest* wins.

Building an advocacy network is the board game you've been given to play to determine who gets the job in the modern workplace, so we need to figure it out as quickly as possible. The good news, again, is that very few people have learned how to play this board game yet, so any shortcomings you may have had from a traditional qualification standpoint matter less now than they ever would have before—employers now have a *new* fair way to evaluate you!

Recall that hiring managers get hundreds of resumes overnight for jobs they post online—too many for them to review, especially when they have projects they have to complete to keep *their* jobs (projects that do not include finding the perfect candidate for their a current opening). They therefore are in satisficing mode; finding a safe (good enough) candidate fast is better than finding a (possibly nonexistent) perfect candidate slowly.

Therefore, informationals are absolutely necessary for getting onto a target employer's internal referral "call list" when openings arise. You become a known asset who clearly cares enough about the job to make the effort to establish contact, rather than just a nameless person who ships a CV their way.

Though this approach seems indirect to you as a job seeker, it is quite direct for a hiring manager. Why comb through hundreds of candidates when you can start with five to ten preapproved ones first?

So I found Boosters who are willing to do informationals with me—what do I talk to them about?

First off, great job! The goal of this process is to get potential Boosters on the phone to gain their trust, so mission accomplished! There will be many to follow, and soon you will see that they are nothing to be scared of. Furthermore, your performance in informationals dramatically improves even after just one or two iterations.

Informationals are a bit hard to visualize before you actually conduct your first one, but they very predictably break down into three sections (or *movements* as in a symphony, where each section has its own tempo and structure):

Informational Movement #1: Small talk

Informational Movement #2: Questions and answers (Q&A)

Informational Movement #3: Next steps

We cover each of these three movements in more detail in the next chapter, but knowing the structure of the conversation in advance helps you identify research to achieve your dual goals of building rapport and gaining usable information. A majority of the benefits from the research that you learn in this chapter will pay off during Movement #2 of the informational conversation, Q&A.

Please tell me that by "research" you don't mean "learn everything I can about the employer."

Oh dear. If you've gotten advice like this in the past, I'm sorry. It's the worst kind of advice—simple to deliver and impossible to follow. It serves more to stress you out than to actually assist you.

Obviously, you can't learn *everything* about an employer before an informational. Research prior to an informational is indeed critical, but once again, the 80/20 Rule applies. Some pieces of information are far more important than others, so we'll gather 80 percent of *that* information in a fraction of the time it would take to become an "expert" on a particular employer or industry, especially given that the person you'll be speaking to will be far more knowledgeable than you, no matter how much you prepare!

Your contact should be your ultimate source of information— you simply want to gather enough knowledge ahead of time to demonstrate proper respect for the contact's time and to be conversant on any current topics the employer may bring up. In this chapter, I'll teach you how to do this with no more than fifteen minutes of effort.

Remember that your dual goal in this conversation is to build rapport and gain usable information. The focus of this conversation should be entirely on your contact, not on you. A selfless informational interviewer is the best informational interviewer. Why? Because selfless informational interviewers spend the most time getting to know their contacts, which reassures them that you'll likely do the same with anyone (especially more senior people) they pass you on to later, ensuring that their professional reputation is protected.

You do not have an infinite amount of time to conduct research on your employers prior to an informational meeting, however. In fact, you may recall how strenuously I've advised you *against* research earlier in this process because of its poor return on effort. Once that informational conversation is scheduled, *then* it is time to conduct more in-depth research.

What research do I need to collect in order to reap 80 percent of the benefit in 20 percent of the time?

The research consists of two parts—external preparation and internal preparation. The external preparation, or information about the company, should take only about fifteen minutes, and its main purpose is to get you conversant on issues likely to be important to the employee you'll be speaking to. The internal preparation, or readiness for questions your informational interviewer is likely to ask *you*, may take longer depending on how much interview practice you've had to date.

What external preparation do I need to do?

At a minimum, you should check three references prior to any informational meeting:

- Investor relations pages on an employer's website

- Headlines on the front page of the employer's website

- Google results for recent employer headlines (and informational interviewers themselves)

The investor relations pages of target employers' websites may seem intimidating at first, but they are a goldmine of information for informationals. Put simply, the purpose of these sections is to entice people with money to find their company exciting enough to invest in them, so the employers themselves will often do your work for you, highlighting reasons the employer is worthy of support yet identifying areas of concern and how they are preparing to address them.

Some of my favorite resources you'll find on these pages are (1) annual reports and 10-K forms, where the CEO of the company summarizes the "state of the union" for the firm, and (2) the company's quarterly results conference calls, where a company representative discusses the SWOT analysis of a company (SWOT stands for Strengths, Weaknesses, Opportunities, and Threats) in very straightforward language. Press releases of major initiatives and recent news headlines including the company will also be highlighted here.

That being said, Google is always an option as well and one that takes even less time than navigating the investor relations page. Just Googling the company's name and "trends" gives you a good approximation of what that employer is facing right now (often directly leading you to the employer's investors relations page anyway!).

These days most employers—those who regularly update their websites, at least—tend to put positive headlines on the front page of their website. That is why I recommend looking there next. You want to make sure you're aware of any recent product launches, new facility openings, or promotional campaigns. Several times I've heard nightmare stories from students who went confidently into an informational meeting only to immediately be stumped by the question, "Did you see our big headline this week?" That's a bad start. The good news is that employers tend to make their good news very easy to find on their website. Then you can at least mention something positive the employer announced recently, even if it's not the specific headline your interviewer wants to speak about.

Finally, on the flip side, you'll want to Google headlines about this prospective employer to make sure you're aware of any problem areas they may be facing right now, such as recent layoffs, turmoil in leadership, or product failures. Although raising such issues would demonstrate that you have done some research on the employer, it puts your interviewers in an uncomfortable position: they may feel pressured to speak negatively about the company. This awkwardness will (rightly) be attributed to you, the job seeker, for asking the embarrassing question, which will lead them to believe you might do the same if they were to refer you to a colleague for another informational. Therefore, the point of checking for negative news about the company is to ensure you steer clear of it. An ounce of prevention. . . .

If you see no negative headlines, then I recommend revising your search to focus on any interesting headlines in major publications that have been posted within the past year.

Before you leave Google, search on your informational interviewer's name and company and see what information is publicly available. This is just good due diligence, potentially giving you an overview of the person's media appearances, for example, or some sense of activities outside of work you may be able to use as an icebreaker.

Finally, be sure to review the contact's LinkedIn profile, whenever applicable. You don't have to memorize the contents, but be familiar with their previous employers and schools. Pay special attention to any information you find in the "Articles & activity" section should one be visible to you; this information will give you a sense of what professional (and possibly even personal) topics your contact is actively discussing at the moment.

Should I mention that I Googled my interviewer before our conversation, or does that risk making me look like a stalker?

It depends on what information you plan to reveal that you found. Some of it is totally appropriate to mention directly, some of it is not. Here's information that is fair game to mention in an informational interview:

- LinkedIn profile information

- Biographical information on the employer's website

- Interviews the contact may have conducted with news organizations, magazines, or industry blogs

Here's information that you should *not* mention having found via Google:

- Nonprofessional media mentions (for example, marriage announcements or charity activity)

- Info gleaned from social media (Facebook, Twitter, Instagram, etc.), unless that social media is professionally focused

- Anything negative

That said, establishing rapport with your interviewer is critical, and identifying a shared passion is an excellent way to do so. Therefore, let's discuss a strategy for how to gracefully accomplish this when you're unsure of the appropriateness of your potential icebreaker.

Let's say you Google an employee with whom you are about to have an informational meeting, and the only result you find is an interview she did with a local newspaper about why she's continued to run marathons for over a decade.

This is a great potential route to rapport with your interviewer if you also enjoy distance running. However, bringing up this article is risky. Some interviewers may not mind that you found that article online and brought it up, being very happy to chat at length about a topic so close to their hearts. However, other interviewers may be creeped out that you brought up an obscure article that clearly implies you Google-stalked them in order to try to establish rapport. So the potential value of mentioning this article is unclear—it could work for or against you.

Therefore, the ideal strategy is to find a way to broach that topic (a fondness for distance running) without mentioning the article. The best way to do this is to dangle that possible connection out to your contact when you are inevitably asked, "Tell me about yourself." If you enjoy running, mention it as an addendum to your story, concluding your career path with, "In addition, my hobbies include yoga and training for my first half-marathon." This allows the interviewer a graceful opening to share her own passion for running with you if she so desires.

Remember, your contacts don't want this conversation to be awkward either, so they will seek to find common ground with you early on. Including some personal information in your background story—especially if you have reason to believe they share similar hobbies—is a courtesy to them, offering a topic that both of you can use to break the ice.

They may choose not to, however—not wishing to get personal at all but preferring to focus on your professional interests. I've had some colleagues who are wonderful people but simply do not like sharing personal information. In this case, it's far better that your mention of hobbies disappears into the ether and the focus shifts back to professional concerns.

Is any more external preparation necessary?

No, that's it, and the best part is that all three of the listed references can be checked in fifteen minutes. Spending more time than that can actually backfire.

Job seekers who over-research in advance of informationals tend to feel the need to show off what they learned, despite the fact that the employer contact is the sole subject matter expert on the call—this can come across as boastful or self-centered. Keep in mind that your best source of information is the contact who's agreed to speak to you. That said, it is your responsibility to create a list of questions that make wise use of their time—questions that either build rapport or help you acquire usable information (or both). The key is to avoid asking them anything you can find on the internet, and that's why the TIARA Framework, which we cover in the next chapter, is such a helpful guide. Before we discuss that, however, we need to discuss *internal preparation*.

What internal preparation do I need to do for informational meetings?

Informationals usually start off with easy small talk, but you need to be prepared to answer the Big Four—four questions so frequently asked during any interview (informational or otherwise) that they get their own nickname.

Even though I explicitly said in the introduction that this is not a book about interviewing, given how commonly the Big Four appear during informationals, job seekers must be prepared for them. Therefore, I will address just these four items, because you often must navigate them effectively during an informational in order to get that first "formal" interview. Here are the Big Four:

1. Tell me about yourself (aka "Walk me through your resume").

2. Why do you want to work for our organization?

3. Why do you want to work in this role?

4. Why do you want to work in this sector/industry?

The Big Four give interviewers a few baseline measures with which they can compare you, apples to apples, with other job search candidates. Interviewers find it incredibly hard to compare one person's advertising accomplishments, for example, to another person's data science accomplishments.

Thus interviewers, seeking to be fair, are likely to assume that all candidates' accomplishments are roughly equivalent—they all made it to the interview, right? This assumption frees them from a lot of decision anxiety about how to value dissimilar backgrounds and allows them to focus more on presentation, which they are better able (and thus prefer) to judge. Behavioral economists call this *substitution bias*—a tendency to evaluate items based on what is observable rather than on what is important, especially when what is important is harder to observe.

If this behavior sounds familiar, it should. Substitution bias is the same rationalizing logic a hiring manager uses to ignore the hundreds of CVs received online for an open position, as we discussed in this book's introduction. It would be unfair to look at only some of them, and there's not enough time to review them all. Thus they cherry-pick the easiest-to-defend selections—people who worked in the space before or who attended the best-regarded schools.

However, the Big Four questions elicit candidate answers that *can* be directly compared. There is nothing background-specific about why candidates want what they want. The credibility of these four answers is therefore especially important, because poor performance here may encourage lazier interviewers to rule you out right away, saving their energy for candidates able to effectively answer these three very fair and fundamental questions.

So how do I answer the Big Four?

I could write a book on this topic alone! But that would be overkill. However, a pamphlet would be insufficient. Thus, I could write somewhere between a pamphlet and a book on this topic alone.

So I . . . did?

I told you this book would not cover interviewing in order to keep it focused on the task at hand, but because I kept getting questions from adherents (after the original edition of 2HJS came out) for how to apply the 2HJS ethos to other elements of the job search,

I compiled the frameworks I've developed over the past decade for everything from interviewing (including the Big Four), resumes, cover letters, negotiations, and more into a companion to *The 2-Hour Job Search*. Visit 2hourjobsearch.com for more information on this follow-up book.

That said, I'll give you brief summaries for each of these questions here so you at least have a plan of attack should these arise in your informationals, which they occasionally will.

The first of the Big Four—"Tell me about yourself"—is the most common for informational meetings and usually the first one. The recruiter's goal here is to form rapport with you and simultaneously try to assess why your path to their organization today makes sense. The maximum duration of this story (and of all of your interview answers, in fact) should be two minutes. Packing all of your life story into two minutes is impossible, but it's entirely feasible if you focus on the good stuff—the whys rather than the whats of your story, which usually means covering the transitions of your life—which are the parts the recruiter cares about.

I created a framework that will keep you on track for either version of this question. It's called the FIT model—Favorite part, Insight gained, and Transition made. Essentially, you describe each stage of your journey in chronological order (since that order is intuitive and easy for listeners to follow) with its own FIT statement, devoting a separate FIT to each promotion and/or combining similar roles into a single FIT statement as necessary to ensure you can finish your answer in two minutes. Here is an example of a FIT statement in action:

In college I studied chemical engineering. My favorite part (F) of chemical engineering was using rigorous logic to break complex problems into smaller, simpler pieces. However, I wanted to apply that rigorous logic to a wider variety of challenges than chemical engineering allowed (I), so upon graduation, I decided to transition into strategy consulting (T).

Start wherever your unique story starts. For some of us that's our first job, for others it's college, and for still others it's a formative childhood experience. Barring a formative childhood experience, I'd recommend that most twenty-somethings start with high school or college interests, thirty-somethings start with college or their first job or two, and more experienced professionals start later than that.

The key point is that this is your life story; you *must* enjoy telling it. Also, make sure it's actually a story—where one event leads logically to the next—rather than an out-loud recitation of your CV. This makes your information more memorable and entertaining, since stories are vastly more interesting than facts alone. Make it engaging, logical, and easy to follow, and don't be afraid to admit mistakes in your career along the way. In interviews, I appreciate when candidates acknowledge mistakes in their past—that vulnerability makes me confident they will disclose any future mistakes they may make on the job and suggests an openness to taking feedback, because they know they aren't perfect.

Note also that while "walk me through your resume" appears to be an entirely different question, it is still to your advantage to answer it using FIT, exactly as you would if asked to "tell me about yourself." The motivations behind your job changes and promotions are far more engaging—especially during the rapport-focused early questions of an informational—than tedious laundry lists of your former responsibilities that bore all parties involved.

Finally, be prepared to mention any particularly unique or important hobbies or community involvement. Remember, the primary goal of this interview is to form rapport. If asking your interviewer questions during the small-talk phase doesn't naturally result in rapport development, disclosing personal information in the hope that your interviewer will reciprocate is another way to possibly kick-start a connection.

What about the other three of the Big Four?

"Why are you interested in our organization?" "Why are you interested in this role? And "Why are you interested in our function/industry?" These are less common in informational meetings, but they do appear. Ideally, what you learn in the informational meeting will make these questions much easier to answer in an actual interview for two main reasons: first, you are getting insider information rather than information from the internet; and second (and more important), you can *source* your assertions.

If a tech company has a reputation for a work-hard-play-hard environment, it's one thing to say, "I want to work for your tech company because of its work-hard-play-hard culture." That may be true, but you may get a "Tell me more about that" or "How do you know that's true?" in response. If you're relying on rumors or reputation alone, your weak research will be noted.

Ideally, you'll have done an informational meeting in advance of your actual interview, so your answer can become, "I spoke to one of your product managers, Catherine Kelly, a couple of weeks ago. I asked her what her favorite part of working for your firm was, and she mentioned how much she enjoyed the firm's 'work-hard-play-hard' environment. That really resonated with me." Your interviewer may disagree with the work-hard-play-hard sentiment, but he won't actually be disagreeing *with you*. He can take that disagreement up with Catherine Kelly. Regardless, you demonstrate that you did your due diligence and managed to name-drop a referral you developed along the way—two wins for the price of one!

In short, just be sure that your answers are specific, relevant, and informed. If you want something more specific, I currently recommend a formula called REC when answering "Why?" questions, where REC stands for **R**eason-**E**vidence-**C**onnection. The Reason is your top-line reason itself. The Evidence is supporting info that demonstrates your assertion is valid. The Connection acknowledges the *employer's* needs rather than yours—they are the ultimate "customer" of your answers, so it's critical (and oft forgotten) to translate your preferences into a benefit to the employer to whom you are currently speaking when the benefit is not immediately apparent.

Create a REC statement for up to three points that you want to highlight during your two-minute answer. For example, if you are asked why tech appeals to you as an industry:

Why are you drawn to technology?

REASON: *The first reason is my love of gadgets. I have been fascinated by gadgets and new technologies ever since I was a child.*

EVIDENCE: *When a lot of my peers were playing with Legos, I gravitated toward computers and electronics stores to see the latest and greatest technology; this passion has followed me into adulthood, where I am typically the first among my friends to know about and experience new products and services.*

CONNECTION: *My fascination with the industry and my constant consumption of news about it from sources ranging from* Wired *to* Fast Company *to* Reddit *gives me confidence I can quickly gain expertise on any product I might manage in the future.*

Note that the connection, while appropriate for job interviews, is usually not appropriate for informationals—it may be viewed as overly aggressive or too sales-y given that your conversation is ostensibly about information and advice rather than jobs.

However, having a connection *prepared* is important, because contacts may follow up with a question like, "How do you think your passion for technology might help you as a product manager?" to gauge your thoughtfulness. In those cases, it's always good to have connections ready (for example, "My familiarity with terminology and recent trends could help me more readily gain the trust of the programmers on my cross-functional teams").

Is that really *all* the preparation I need to do for an informational meeting?

Obviously, you can research an employer forever, but doing more than necessary is an inefficient use of time. You hit the point of diminishing returns quickly. You are looking for lively conversation topics during your research, not complex "stump your contact" questions. Contacts at your target employers are people too, so they prefer knowing answers to not knowing answers (and thus losing face in front of a new acquaintance). Plus, highly specific questions tend to be based on objective facts rather than easy-to-conjure opinions, which can make them risky for you to ask, tedious for the contact to answer, and not all that helpful even when you can get a correct response.

In other words, it's a lose-meh situation, so the Boot Theory (see page 124) once again applies. When you "win" you don't really feel better, but when you "lose" you will definitely feel worse. Simply refuse that bet, especially given the extensive effort creating these questions so often involves.

Furthermore, contacts will then associate you with awkward and tiresome conversations (fundamental attribution error again; even if your contact should have known the answer to your technical question, they'll still likely blame you for asking rather than blame themselves for not knowing the answer!). This makes them very unlikely to internally refer you out of concern that you'll similarly embarrass their colleague.

As you'll see in the next chapter, the questioning algorithm in the TIARA Framework is designed to never stump your contact—most of the questions can be answered just as well by a first-year analyst as by a thirty-year veteran of an organization. Plus, they tend to be fun and engaging to answer in general.

If my contact never asks me any of the Big Four, should I bring them up myself?

No, there is no need! If someone spends the entire conversation talking about themselves (and this does happen from time to time), they are either a Booster who lost themselves in the flattering conversation you gave them—and thus will want to return the favor by doing anything they can for you subsequently—or an Obligate who didn't want to form a relationship with you in the first place . . . but may feel obligated to, following your selfless conversation. Either way, you did the best you could under the circumstances!

What if my interviewer turns this into an impromptu job interview?

Outside of a few specific sectors (see Time Out #6, opposite), this thankfully doesn't happen very often. However, if an interview starts, you interview. After all, that's what the ultimate end goal of your networking was in the first place! Doing your best in the moment may be less than ideal, but asking to postpone the conversation (that you requested, mind you) until you've had additional time to prepare tends to turn out very poorly. Thus, attempting to postpone the conversation at that point is not recommended!

Banker Beware!

Certain sectors are notorious for allowing job seekers to set up informational meetings but then converting those informationals into actual job interviews without notice.

Investment banking (IB) provides by far the best-known examples of this behavior. Certain contacts simply prefer to spend that time actually interviewing you—complete with questions about the stock market's performance that day, several stocks you'd recommend right now, and so on—rather than allowing you to ask them questions.

When pursuing a career in investment banking, prepare for informational interviews, but also be ready for that informational to turn into a real interview.

Thankfully, IB is the exception rather than the rule in this respect. When it does happen outside of IB, it tends to be with smaller employers that lack standard interview processes. Therefore, you may want to err on the side of caution if your area of focus includes the small employer–heavy social impact or start-up spaces in particular!

TROUBLESHOOTING

What if I live far away from my contact? Do I need to conduct informationals in person?

No, not at all. Expect that most of your informationals will be by phone, particularly since not all of your contacts will be comfortable meeting a stranger for the first time in person.

The best way to gauge a contact's comfort with meeting in person is when they respond to your 6-Point Email; reply with an offer to chat by phone or meet in person, whichever they'd prefer. They will then typically opt in to the format with which they are more comfortable.

continued

TROUBLESHOOTING

Don't worry if a local contact opts to chat with you by phone rather than in person—it really is easier to fit a phone call in during business hours, and I find that the success rate at converting informationals to referrals does not vary based on whether the meeting is in person or by phone.

I recommend putting a maximum commute of ninety minutes one way to meeting with a contact in person if they are amenable to it, unless your industry has a norm where in-person meetings are expected (Wall Street jobs come to mind here). Your time is precious, as are the costs of commuting (monetary and otherwise). Any further than ninety minutes and the travel begins to distract you from the higher value-added activity of doing more informationals.

Regarding the physical logistics of conducting an informational by phone, try to use a land-based phone line whenever possible to ensure good reception. However, many job seekers have only their cell phones and thus lack easy access to a landline. In those cases, simply choose to conduct the call in a quiet, private place with very good reception. (If you have no choice but to conduct the call from a coffee shop, choose a quiet one.) Do not put your contact on speakerphone (since you will be harder to understand) or, at the very least, apologize that circumstances have forced you to do so and mention why.

If you have the luxury of being able to conduct the call from a private room and space allows, I further recommend taking the call standing up at a counter (your voice will sound more confident) and ideally in front of a mirror so you remember to smile while you speak (your voice will sound more likable—this old sales trick genuinely does make a difference, and people absolutely can tell the difference!). Lastly, I recommend taking your notes by hand rather than by computer. Your contacts will be able to hear you typing, but they won't know if you're taking notes or messaging your roommate about the call you're stuck on, so spare them that uncertainty!

TROUBLESHOOTING

What if I can't find much information about one of my target employers because it is a very small company and/or privately held?

If you have access to a library, again, see what resources they have access to and may recommend. (For example, the Fuqua Library pointed me to a database called PrivCo, which focuses exclusively on providing research on privately owned companies.)

That said, again, your best sources of information about an organization are the actual informational interviewers themselves. Plus, smaller and private organizations will be well aware that extensive information about them is not readily available to the general public.

As long as you spend fifteen minutes trying to complete the external preparation recommended earlier, you have done your due diligence. This story may even prove to be an effective icebreaker, letting your contacts know how their insights are *especially* appreciated, given how little you were able to uncover during your research for this conversation. There are secretive companies out there, so the fact that you know their employer falls into this category is itself an insight.

## CHAPTER 9

DISCUSS

Okay, now that I'm prepared to answer questions my target employer contacts might ask me, what am *I* supposed to ask *them*?

Recall from the preceding chapter that the purpose of the informational meeting is to both form rapport and gain usable information. Also remember that informationals are generally conducted in three distinct movements: (1) small talk, (2) questions and answers, and (3) next steps. Before we discuss how to optimize each of these movements in detail, however, let's take a moment to learn about the Ben Franklin effect, otherwise known as "why informational meetings work."

What is the Ben Franklin effect?

The Ben Franklin effect is a psychology concept related to the "foot-in-the-door" technique, a sales tactic that aims to convince someone to make a major purchase or behavioral change by requesting a series of small concessions rather than a complete commitment all at once. The Ben Franklin effect, however, uses favor requests, rather than concessions, to achieve the same desired effect.

In Ben Franklin's autobiography, he outlines this strategy—an insight he identified in the 1700s. After being unanimously elected clerk of the General Assembly in Philadelphia in 1736, he won reelection the following year, but only after an affluent and influential assembly newcomer made a long speech in support of Ben's opponent. Ben wanted to nip this resistance in the bud, as he sensed this newcomer's influence would only grow with time. I'll let him tell you what happened next in his own words:

> I therefore did not like the opposition of this new member, who was a gentleman of fortune and education, with talents that were likely to give him, in time, great influence in the House, which, indeed, afterwards happened. I did not, however, aim at gaining his favour by paying any servile respect to him, but, after some time, took this other method. Having heard that he had in his library a certain very scarce and curious book, I wrote a note to him, expressing my desire of perusing that book, and requesting he would do me the favour of lending it to me for a few days. He sent it immediately, and I return'd it in about a week with another note, expressing strongly my sense of the favour. When we next met in the House, he spoke to me (which he had never done before), and with great civility; and he ever after manifested a readiness to serve me on all occasions, so that we became great friends, and our friendship continued to his death. This is another instance of the truth of an old maxim I had learned, which says, "He that has once done you a kindness will be more ready to do you another, than he whom you yourself have obliged."[1]

Remarkably, Ben Franklin turned an adversary into an ally by asking him for a favor!

This is backed up by a 1969 study in which participants were awarded prize money by a researcher based on their performance in an intellectual contest. Participants were then randomly split into three groups:

- One-third of the group was approached by the researcher, who asked them to return the prize money, saying he had self-funded the study and was now running short.

- One-third of the group was approached by a secretary, who asked them to return their prize money, saying it was from the psychology department, for which funds were now running short.

- One-third of the group was not approached at all—this was the control group.

Each group was then surveyed about their feelings toward the researcher. Unsurprisingly, the group approached by the secretary to return the money liked the researcher less than the control group did. However, the group the researcher approached himself to ask that the funds be returned, liked him more than the control group did! A personal request for a favor in this case increased liking, whereas an impersonal request decreased it.[2]

Counterintuitively, allowing someone to do you a favor is an incredibly powerful way to gain their loyalty. If I were to go on vacation and ask you to mow my lawn while I was away, I would obviously be indebted to you. You did me a favor, and I "owe you one." What is less obvious is that—by "allowing" you to do me the favor of mowing my lawn—I've increased the likelihood that you will perform further (and greater) favors for me in the future.

It is this insight, first delineated hundreds of years ago, that the approach to informationals you're now learning builds upon. In an informational meeting, you are asking someone for a small favor of time and information. By not returning this favor immediately (as Ben Franklin pointedly refrained from doing), you increase the amount your contact likes you, as well as the likelihood they will help you again in the future. Therefore, informational meetings should be viewed as both short- and long-term investments.

Maximizing the long-term benefit of informationals is the subject of chapter 10. Maximizing the short-term benefit is our topic in this chapter, and that means conducting effective informational meetings. The first "movement," paving the way for Q&A and next steps, is conducting good small talk.

Movement #1: Small talk

Is good small talk something that can be created? Or is it more a matter of luck?

To be sure, small talk comes naturally to some and not to others. If small talk has always come naturally to you, just keep doing you and know that my jealousy knows no bounds. However, if you're like me and small talk doesn't come naturally, we need to put a little more thought into this part of the process.

First of all, I hope you know by now that I don't really believe in luck! I almost believe in "creating your own luck," but that's still too random for my taste. Instead, I believe in maximizing the probability of desired outcomes.

Ultimately, nothing in the job search is guaranteed, but having the right plan in place in advance gives you the highest chance of success. The probability of creating good small talk is no different, and since it didn't come naturally to me, in my own previous job searches I had to find ways to make it systematic. It's far more possible than you might think.

So how do I maximize my chance of creating good small talk?

In short, take a genuine interest in the other person. *Interested is interesting.*

The easiest way to do this is to give the person a chance to talk about whatever he or she wants to talk about—especially initially. The first rule of facilitation in any context is "follow the energy."

Therefore, if your contact becomes more energetic in response to a question, stay with it for a follow-up question or two.

Follow-up questions are very effective for building likability. A Harvard study found that people who asked follow-up questions during conversations (in addition to the three other types: (1) introductory questions like "How are you?;" (2) mirror questions like "Fine. How are you?;" and (3) full-switch questions, where you move on to an entirely new topic) were considered more likable than those who did not.[3] If your contact does not become more energetic in response, move on to the next question.

Again, if you're already good at small talk, keep doing what you've always naturally done, but if you've ever struggled to establish small talk, you may wish to borrow my three-question algorithm for small talk.

I knew you'd have one!

Really? After a couple hundred pages I'm becoming predictable?

Indeed, I have a small-talk algorithm. Whenever I'm trying to get a conversation going in an informational (or pretty much any other context—my past first dates may wish to skip this part . . .), I open with these three questions.

1. How is your day going so far?"

    This is a temperature-check question. It seems basic, but I am looking for a specific piece of information: are my contacts chatty or all business? If they offer a businesslike "Fine. And yours?" I reciprocate with "Fine as well" . . . and move to the next question.

    However, if they offer any extraneous information above and beyond what was necessary to answer a very simple question ("Oh, it's been a crazy morning. My dog got sick, so I had to race into work to make it here on time!"), I'll ask an appropriate follow-up question about that extraneous information ("Oh no! Is your dog okay?"), since extraneous information is a signal they are trying to help me out—maybe not consciously, but subconsciously in an effort to avoid an awkward conversation. More importantly, though, it shows the other person that I'm genuinely listening.

2. "So what's been your path to joining <organization>?"

In effect, I am asking the "Tell me about yourself" question before the contact can ask me. This again gives me a sense for how personal or professional the contact prefers to be. Does the contact mention hobbies, or is it all work-based? Furthermore, it gives me a sense for what duration of answer they find appropriate, since manners dictate that this question will typically be reflected right back; that's why it's important to have prepared your answer to "Tell me about yourself" in advance!

That said, a full FIT-format answer won't always be appropriate! Simply mirror their behavior: If your contacts take thirty seconds to answer, you take thirty seconds. If they take two minutes, you take two minutes. If they take five minutes . . . you'll still just take two minutes. Remember, two minutes max for all your answers! Your contact is the star of this show, and when they're talking, you're building likability.

More generally, keep the tone consistent with theirs. If they are introspective in answering this question, absolutely follow suit (and FIT will make this easy). If they stick closer to the surface, do likewise and try to get more energy from them through follow-up questions about their path or through our third question.

3. "What are you working on right now?"

This question demonstrates that I have a sincere interest in the type of work the contact actually does. Plus, if a person hasn't given you energy thus far, it's likely because they either have work on their mind or simply prefer discussing professional topics—either way, again, it's easier to run forward (from rapport building to shop talk) than backward (from shop talk back to rapport building). Typically, if the previous two questions haven't garnered any energy, this one most certainly will.

If you have gotten good information from questions #1 and #2, you are not obligated to ask question #3! Feel free to roll right from your contact's path (or your own, if they reflect the question back to you) into your reasons for calling them today. Just know that question #3 (or something similar, like "Is this a busy time of year for you?") is an option if the person seems distracted or more interested in the here and now than history.

During the small-talk phase of the conversation, you will spend your time mirroring the topics and demeanor of your contact. In this phase, your primary goal is to build rapport (you may also gain usable information here, but that is less critical). So speak about hobbies if your interviewer does, and avoid them otherwise.

It helps to think of this less as an asking algorithm and more as a listening algorithm. When you are spending energy trying to think of what to ask next, you have less energy to genuinely hear what your contact is telling you. Therefore, if you have a script—even if you just start with one that you quickly veer away from should an organic conversation take off and lead you in an unexpected direction—you are more likely to ask good follow-up questions.

What if my contact and I find we share a common interest and they want to continue talking about that?

By all means, do so! You're forming rapport, which is the primary goal of this conversation. The usable information can always be collected later, but rapport (which usually precedes advocacy) has to happen initially or it is unlikely to occur.

Even if you tap into a passion of theirs that you don't share, you can take a genuine interest and still gain a lot of the same benefit from it. A common piece of conventional wisdom for international students going to school in the US is to learn about US professional sports, since that is a topic that often comes up in small-talk situations.

That, however, is incredibly challenging to actually do. A surface-level familiarity typically won't be sufficient to engage in meaningful small talk on the subject, and a deep familiarity would require dozens of hours of effort for a topic for which you may have no passion whatsoever! Thus, if you don't follow sports, ask instead about *their* passion for a particular sport.

For example, let's say I ask someone how their day was going, and they said they were tired today since they were up late watching the sillyball match. Neither I nor you know anything about sillyball, since sillyball doesn't exist. However, I can still ask logical follow-up questions like, "I've never heard of sillyball. How does sillyball work? How did you discover sillyball? Have you ever played sillyball? What skills make someone a good sillyball player?" and so on. Not only will my contact feel heard (building likability), but I will have learned something that may prove useful in the future if I ever meet another sillyball fan.

More generally, just because you don't *know* sports doesn't mean you can't *talk* sports, or any other topic for that matter, as long as you take a genuine interest in the other person's energy for it. And you'll find authentically engaging on your lack of knowledge will be much more rewarding and effective than inauthentically engaging on very limited knowledge.

So whether you're bonding over rescue dogs, being raised in a large family, or being long-suffering Cleveland Browns fans—or you're just learning about the existence of sillyball for the very first time—*follow the energy*. This algorithm for small talk is not foolproof, but it gives those of us to whom small talk does not come naturally a structure for systematically attempting to break the ice and establish rapport!

How long should I stay in the small-talk phase before moving on to Movement #2, Q&A?

Although there is no exact answer to this question, given that your main strategy is to follow the energy shown by the interviewer, I would say, expect the small-talk phase of the conversation to last about five minutes, but if the energy is high, feel free to go to ten minutes. You can bridge this transition—particularly when you sense the energy starting to flag—with a comment like, "Thank you again for making time for me. I did prepare some questions for you, so may I ask you those now?" The questioning algorithm that follows is where the TIARA Framework gets its name.

Movement #2: Questions and Answers

Why is the framework called TIARA?

TIARA is an acronym for the five topics you'll cover during the Q&A portion of the informational: Trends, Insights, Advice, Resources, and Assignments. This questioning algorithm maximizes the likelihood of having a successful informational meeting that both builds rapport and provides usable information.

Another benefit of the TIARA acronym is that it's easy to remember on short notice, because occasionally informationals can occur without any warning whatsoever! Have you ever been seated at a table of strangers at a conference luncheon or wedding reception, where making conversation is pretty much required? All of these situations are potential informational meetings. TIARA will actually help you negotiate these situations as well. (Furthermore, because these people are strangers, they're perfect candidates to practice your technique on because you have nothing to lose.)

Consider TIARA to be the Heimlich Maneuver of informational interviewing—a replicable, reliable routine for stressful situations, TIARA guides you through the process of earning a person's trust and fondness, enabling you to conduct an informational on a moment's notice (even without research, when necessary).

Is a "questioning algorithm" really necessary?

Necessary? No. Incredibly helpful? Yes, especially if you've never known what to ask before. Knowing what questions to ask and in what order dramatically improves your ability to turn informationals into job interviews. Furthermore, *knowing* you know that information greatly reduces your anxiety about this step of the process.

Can't I just be direct and ask them, "Can you help me find a job?"

No, unfortunately. Although this approach would be efficient for you, it scares away potential advocates who won't feel comfortable giving you any meaningful help until you've earned their trust and fondness.

How and why does TIARA work?

The fundamental thesis of TIARA is that you'll begin the conversation by treating your contacts as experts in their field, but over the course of the informational, your questions will shift in tone and depth so you frame your contact more personally as a mentor, maximizing the chance that you'll turn this stranger into an advocate within a single conversation.

So, at a high level, TIARA flows like this:

- Trends   Expert
- Insights
- Advice   Mentor
- Resources
- Assignments

Before I describe TIARA in more detail, let's do a quick thought experiment. Put yourself in the position of the contact. Imagine you are at work and you get a call from Jimmy, a job seeker from your hometown. After some small talk, his first question to you is, "What do you recommend I do to get a job with your employer?"

You don't really know Jimmy yet, so exposing your personal network to him without knowing him better seems risky. It would reflect poorly on you if you passed him on to a colleague and he was similarly awkward and forward in that conversation (a fair assumption). Plus, you aren't thinking particularly creatively at this point in the conversation—you're still probably thinking logically about the deadlines and emails you put on hold to take Jimmy's call.

In short, Jimmy's request is too abrupt. He's made only a cursory attempt to get to know you, so you in turn are likely to make only a cursory attempt to *help* him. Something is missing here between small talk and a request for advice. This job seeker is attempting to turn you into his mentor without first acknowledging your expertise.

Simply saying, "I acknowledge your expertise—how do I get a job with your employer?" won't cut it either. Jimmy needs to give you a chance to show off some of that expertise before asking for your mentorship. You could be completely clueless or a total maniac, for all he knows! Just as you wouldn't trust someone offering to buy your car sight unseen, you certainly wouldn't trust a job seeker who asks for your advice without kicking your tires first. The best way to probe your expertise is with some open-ended yet engaging questions about your professional experience. This increases both trust and likability.

Small talk (Movement #1 of our informational) gave us a systematic way to warm contacts up before asking anything of them. Using TIARA for Q&A (Movement #2 of our informational) ensures that any requests we *do* make are nonthreatening and aligned with our previously declared focus on gathering information and insight—not asking for a job. Our contacts, if treated properly, may *offer* us job search assistance, but that is their prerogative and shouldn't be explicitly requested (at least not in this conversation, anyway).

Fun and Flattering

A common yet terrible question I hear novice job seekers ask in informational settings is, "What's the corporate culture like at your firm?" This is basically the worst.

This isn't flattering or fun to answer. It's just painful. This information is available online, and you'll bore your contact as they run through a list of positive qualities that appear on the company website. (Or worse, they'll do what you should have done and Google it.)

So how can we take "What's the corporate culture like at your firm?" and change it slightly to make it fun and flattering? Any ideas? If not, here's some guidance.

To make a question flattering, ask for opinions rather than facts (so your contacts can answer with 100 percent certainty regardless of the question) and inquire about positive topics rather than negative ones.

To make a question fun to answer, ask for superlatives— their *best* example, *favorite* experience, *most interesting* project. This removes the temptation for them to "laundry-list" all possible answers (as they would for "What experiences/ projects have you enjoyed?"), losing energy as they add one more similar item to the running tally.

So let's try one more time before I give you the answer— how can you make the question, "What's the corporate culture like at your firm?" both fun and flattering?

Answer: Simply change it to "What's your favorite part of the corporate culture at your firm?" It's flattering since they are experts on their own opinion of the culture—not the company's culture at large—and it's fun to answer because you're challenging their creativity to pick the *one* thing they like best rather than challenging their memory to list all the positive qualities of the culture. A strong, well-considered favorite has the added benefit of invoking a greater level of energy in response as well, providing richer fodder for follow-up questions (and thus likability) in the process.

So, what sorts of questions should I ask during each of the five steps of TIARA?

Remember that we don't want to "stump the contact," nor do we want to spend a lot of time digging up research-based questions that are tedious to answer and may be seen as transparent attempts to impress (an approach Ben Franklin would surely frown upon).

The ideal questions for TIARA are both flattering and fun to answer. We see this concept in action in Quickstart Exercise #3 on page 189.

Ideal TIARA questions are open-ended enough to engage the contact creatively yet generic enough to be reusable over multiple conversations (although they will inevitably become more sophisticated over time). Here's another look at TIARA, with a sample question from each step of the informational, to give you an idea of where we're headed:

Trends: "What trend is most impacting your business right now?"

Insights: "What surprises you most about your job?"

Advice: "If you were me, what would you be doing right now to best prepare for a career in this field?"

Resources: "What resources should I be sure to look into next?"

Assignments: "What's been your favorite project so far?"

Now we will look at each step of the TIARA Framework in more detail.

TREND QUESTIONS

Trend (not to be confused with trend*ing*) questions are broad, macro-level industry questions that provide an excellent way to open an informational interview because, whether your contacts are junior or senior employees of their firm, they will readily be able to provide interesting answers that allow them to feel smart. The only difference will be the scope of work that their insights cover. Some good Trend questions are:

- "What trend is most impacting your business right now?"

- "How has your sector changed most since you started?"

- "How do you predict your industry will change most dramatically in the next several years?"

These questions require no research, they make your contact think in a real way, and you can ask these questions of five different employees and receive five different, equally valid answers. The versatility, depth, and durability of these questions make them extremely effective openers. Chief information officers may highlight big-picture technology trends impacting their business, whereas second-year programmers may instead discuss how a new software package is impacting their work team—however, both perspectives are extremely helpful. Plus, these are the types of questions that are likely to make your contact say, "Give me a second to think about that . . . ," which indicates they are truly giving you an original and accurate answer that reflects the best of their expertise and experience, rather than trite, easy answers requiring no thought.

Besides, it's much more fun as an interview subject to discuss what trends you think are most impacting your business than it is to describe your company's corporate culture. People enjoy talking about themselves more than they enjoy talking about their employers. Granted, all these questions are asked in the context of your contact's current employer, but they all focus on getting the contact to give you the best information they can. We want the person to truly engage, and these questions are a great way to do that.

Won't that sort of question seem overly simplistic to an informational interviewer?

It won't unless you have an informational unicorn who enjoys answering Google-able questions more than personal ones. In fact, the simplicity of these questions is what makes them great options for those of you who are new to informational meetings.

How can the answers I get from Trend questions be useful later?

They will make you a better informational interviewer, for starters! While your informational questions may start off basic, your future versions of these questions will become more sophisticated over time. For example, let's say I do an informational with a marketing manager at Kraft on a Monday, and I ask, "What trend, in your opinion, is most impacting your business right now?" In reply, my contact says that rising oil prices have compelled them to overhaul their distribution strategy to minimize fuel costs, which she fears could skyrocket at any moment.

Next, during my informational with General Mills on Wednesday of that same week, instead of asking simply, "What trend is most impacting your business right now?" I can ask the same question in a more credible fashion—for example, "During my research, I've learned that rising oil prices are causing consumer packaged goods companies to overhaul their distribution to save on costs. Are you seeing a similar trend, or is another trend impacting you more seriously right now?"

This is essentially the same question: "What factor is most impacting your business right now?" The only difference is that in the second iteration, I demonstrate some second-level insight—or insight I couldn't have easily gotten off the internet but only learned by asking a professional in the field. This shows the General Mills contact that I've done my homework prior to that conversation and encourages them to raise the bar and give me an even more sophisticated answer, which I can then use to improve future iterations of the question in subsequent informational meetings. It's a virtuous cycle—good information begets further good information.

Remember that the goal here is to keep the contact's energy level high. If they clearly enjoy this line of questioning, stay with it. Ask follow-up questions to their answers; for example, "What's involved in redesigning a distribution strategy, particularly for someone in marketing?"

You may get to ask only one Trend question before the conversation takes off (and it's best never to go with more than two—one is ideal), but once the energy seems to flag slightly, that is your signal to move to the next step in TIARA: Insights.

INSIGHT QUESTIONS

Insight questions are very similar to Trend questions, but they start to become slightly more personal rather than strictly business-related. We want the contact to gradually become more comfortable disclosing personal information to us, and that starts with getting them to share their personal feelings. Here are some good Insight questions:

- "What surprises you most about your job/your employer?"
- "What's the best lesson you've learned thus far on the job?"
- "What's been your best professional decision so far, and why?"
- "If you had to attribute your ten years of success at your employer to one skill or trait, what would it be?" (This is especially effective for more senior or recently promoted contacts, with a good follow-up being, "Is that trait shared by many across the firm, or is it unique and you've adapted it to your advantage?")

Again, these questions do not require research, yet they build rapport with your contact—simply because they are fun to answer. Your contact is the world's foremost expert on their own insights, so they can't be wrong. These questions also require them to activate the creative part of their brain (this will be essential later), which allows you to demonstrate a genuine interest in their experiences and insights. Furthermore, the information you collect here can be incredibly useful, meeting our secondary goal in the informational interview process!

How can the answers I get from Insight questions be useful later?

There are many ways, but the most significant way is that it opens your contact up to further personal disclosure (and ideally empathy) later in the interview, because you've demonstrated a genuine interest in what the contact has to say. In addition, you've kept your word that this conversation would be about the contact's experiences and insights—not a job. The later steps in the TIARA Framework require a high level of trust to be effective, so it's important to take your time during the initial steps.

These answers are also useful during future interviews, both informationals and job interviews. As we learned in chapter 8, the ability to source information is incredibly powerful for establishing credibility. Instead of making a sweeping generalization about this start-up's work-hard-play-hard culture with no tangible proof, being able to attribute that assertion to the current product manager dramatically sets you apart from other candidates. You are a safer pick to advance than one who (1) is less networked at the firm and (2) makes a habit of making assertions without proof.

Similarly, being able to source your information is useful in formal cover letters you may be asked to prepare. (For a more in-depth look at how to create cover letters quickly and easily, visit 2hourjobsearch .com to find more information on my follow-up book.)

Finally, answers to Insight questions are also useful in that they allow you to form a mosaic of the industry, function, and employer you are attempting to join. Particularly for those attempting to change careers, this may save you from a significant career misstep due to misunderstanding the true day-to-day nature of the work or organizations you are pursuing. Career changers will hear different answers every time they ask a particular question from the Insight family, but over time the answers will converge to form very accurate patterns.

When the energy of this question starts to flag, or when you reach the two-thirds mark in your interview, you'll want to move on to the next step of TIARA: Advice.

ADVICE QUESTIONS

By now we've developed some rapport with our contacts and have engaged the creative parts of their brain in the conversation, so this is the time when we start trying to reframe our contacts as mentors rather than simply as experts. Mentors take a long-term interest in the welfare of their mentees, whereas experts may feel their work is "done" once they've imparted their wisdom to you. The onus is on the job seeker to convert the expert into a mentor, because advocates' benefits are not usually imparted immediately, and the Advice phase of TIARA is the best time to attempt this conversion.

Advice questions are actually very similar to Insight questions, except they involve one additional element: empathy. In this part of the conversation, we are actively trying to get our contacts to put themselves in your shoes, convincing them to give us not just vague advice for what we should do next but the actual steps they would take if they themselves were in our position right now. Here are some good examples of Advice questions:

- "If you were me, what's the one thing you'd be doing now to best prepare for a career in this field?"

- "What do you know now that you wish you knew when you were in my position?"

- "If you were me, what would you be doing right now to maximize your chance of breaking into this industry or function?"

- "If you had just been hired into this role, what's the most important thing you'd do in your first thirty days to ensure you got off to the fastest start possible?"

Again, these questions are durable—they can be used over and over without becoming stale, and they do not require extensive research. The biggest mistake job seekers make in the informational meeting process is thinking that the conversation is about themselves (i.e., selling), when it is really about the contact (i.e., learning). The TIARA Framework provides a structure that effectively makes this common mistake impossible, because your contact—not you—will be speaking for the vast majority of the conversation.

The ideal outcome of an informational is that your contact begins to view your job search success (or lack thereof) as a reflection of their own ability to give good guidance and/or be a good mentor. If they actually give you the best advice they can come up with and you execute it all flawlessly (which you will, following the 2HJS Harvest Cycle that we discuss in depth in our next and final chapter) but still fail to find success, you will email them an update on your progress. This update will recap the advice they gave you, how you've followed it, and what results you've achieved, *as well as* solicit further recommendations.

I've heard stories from my students about certain Boosters becoming the job search equivalent of superheroes within their organizations at this point, following up with referrals they (the Boosters) contacted previously to get updates and asking additional coworkers whether they are looking for any solid candidates. Why is this?

Simply put, *nobody likes to think they give bad advice*—this, after all, causes cognitive dissonance, and people will go to great lengths to restore their belief that they are fantastic. In fact, this follow-up request for further recommendations kicks the Ben Franklin effect back in, wherein they invest in you further now, if only to rationalize their previous efforts to help you. Without gaining their empathy for your situation, this is impossible. Your Boosters will need to give you thoughtful advice in order to develop any sense that you are now a mentee of theirs.

How can the answers I get from Advice questions be useful later?

These answers are how we prove to our contacts that we are a safe referral. We do this by showing our contacts that we are the type of candidate who, when given advice by a mentor (in an informational or in any other venue), has the drive to follow that advice and the responsibility to report back the results.

That means it is essential to take excellent notes during this part of the conversation. These notes will be *the* featured element of your first follow-up email after your informational (not to be confused with your thank-you note immediately following the conversation), because they are what will trigger the Ben Franklin effect in the future.

Once the Advice phase of the conversation has run its course, or when you are within a few minutes of the end of your scheduled time allotment, it is time to move to the fourth segment of TIARA: Resources, which includes the single most important question of the entire informational—the Pivot question.

RESOURCE QUESTIONS

We've just finished asking our contact a series of questions designed to make them empathize with our situation so they now better comprehend the challenges of finding employment in a market where "being qualified" alone simply isn't enough.

Resource questions are designed to elicit where your contacts go when they need or want information about their industry, function, or business. These can be people, places, or things. Obviously, we are most interested in people (namely, hiring managers to whom our contact will advocate for us), but we are bound by the promise we made when we reached out to our contact in the first place—that the conversation would be about experience and insight, not jobs.

If the contact offers to *make* the conversation about jobs, however . . . we'll get to that in a minute.

The Resources topic in TIARA always starts with the *Pivot question*:

- "What resources would you recommend I look into next?" and alternatively:

- "What next steps would you recommend for someone in my situation?"

Regardless of how long Trend, Insight, and Advice questions take during your informational meeting, you *must* ask the Pivot question before the conversation ends. This question is what allows you to determine how to wrap up the conversation. Thus the Pivot question is always asked first before any other Resource questions.

Resource questions are designed to determine what sources of potential advantage your contact would leverage if they were in your situation. This ideally involves specific people—referrals. However, we will pursue these very gently. There are other Resource questions available to you, but we'll explore those after we see how our contact responds to the Pivot question.

The Pivot question is purposely vague about the sort of help you're seeking. We can't gracefully ask for handoffs to hiring managers given that we said this conversation was about information and not jobs, but we *can* give interviewers a chance to gracefully offer those handoffs to us, if they are so inclined.

I call this the Pivot question because—depending on your interviewers' answers to it—your conversation will go in one of two directions in Movement #3 on page 208. If they offer you referrals without your asking (expect this to be the exception rather than the norm!), then you've hit the jackpot—you've found a Booster ready and willing to help you move your candidacy along. However, if the contact doesn't offer you such referrals right away (or asks for more specificity about the sort of help you're seeking), then the process of gaining advocacy will take a bit more time and follow-up.

What if my contact offers to connect me to a hiring manager?

This is the ideal scenario—your contact turns out to be a rabid Booster willing to open their network to you right away.

In response to the Pivot, they consider who's the next person you should speak and either offer to connect you personally or give you that person's contact information and grant you permission to use their name as a referral. Either method suffices for your purposes, but you must obligate yourself to following up with your contact in a couple of weeks to let them know how things turn out. *This is absolutely critical.* Set a reminder for yourself (à la the 3B7 Routine) two weeks from the day of that informational so it stays on your radar without your having to think about it.

Earlier I mentioned that one of the quickest ways to alienate Boosters is by not responding quickly (within a business day) when they offer you times for informational interviews. Equally destructive is not following up with Boosters after they agree to help you, leaving your status a complete mystery to them after they put their reputation on the line for you with no personal incentive whatsoever.

This is bad form, but even worse, it allows you no graceful course of action should the referral not respond (and this happens more often than you'd expect). My job seekers who fail to obligate themselves to follow up often find themselves in an uncomfortable situation where they get no response yet have no clear path forward for what to do next. This usually results in weeks of anxiety, culminating in a belated request to your contact asking how you should proceed given their referral didn't respond. This request appears needy, and given how easily you can avoid having to make it, there is simply no excuse for putting yourself in such a stressful and exposed position.

By telling a Booster who just offered you a referral something along the lines of, "Thank you so much! I'll reach out to Wendy immediately, and I'll check back with you in a couple of weeks to let you know what happens," you have your bases covered. If you and the referral connect and have a great conversation, you can let your Booster know this and give them the satisfaction of knowing they helped someone in need.

However, if the referral never responds to your outreach (this assumes you tried twice: once initially and again seven business days later—yes, you set 7B reminders on referral contacts as well, although you do not need to set 3B reminders on them since there is no alternate contact), you have no choice but to update your Booster about the situation, because you swore you would, and keeping your word at all times throughout this process is a must.

This email doesn't have to be negative, though. It could simply be something like this:

> *Thanks again for taking the time to speak to me—that information was very helpful! As promised, I wanted to provide you with an update on my status. Per your suggestion, I reached out to Wendy, but unfortunately we haven't been able to connect. Do you have any suggestions for how to best proceed from here?"*

A message like this carries several benefits. First, it informs your Booster that you did not flake. Without an update from you, they will assume that you—rather than the referral—dropped the ball, so it is critical to inform them that you held up your end of their favor. Second, it gives you a second chance at your Booster's referral with minimal awkwardness—after all, you're just keeping a promise to a Booster rather than complaining about anyone else's shortcomings. Third, it allows your Booster to improvise next steps on your behalf.

Boosters will usually be willing to do more for you than you yourself would be willing to ask, so it is better to defer to their expertise for how to proceed if their referral is unavailable rather than to ask them for a specific action—like to check in with the referral on your behalf. Instead, ask your Booster what they'd recommend for you next—they may then recall that the referral is consumed with launching a new product critical to the firm's success right now, and they will try directing you to someone else (better yet, the hiring manager).

In short, Boosters know best. Defer to their judgment whenever things start going wrong. This shows that you take direction well, know when to defer to experts, and will protect their brand by not "going rogue" when things don't go according to plan.

One quick note before we leave the jackpot scenario—if a Booster writes the email introduction for you and copies you on the message, Reply All within twenty-four hours to express your interest in speaking to that new contact soon. This way, the new contact knows the next move is clearly up to them. In fact, offer in your email to call at a certain time or suggest some times that are good to speak, if that would be convenient for them, to add some urgency to the connection. This confirms for your Booster that you've done your part.

That said, I would shortly thereafter write the Booster a thank-you email (without copying the new contact) for making that connection, again with a promise to follow up with your Booster in a couple of weeks to report on what happened.

So that's the easy scenario. In short, if an informational interviewer appears to be a Booster and gives you a contact right away, follow these steps:

1. Send a thank-you email to the Booster within twenty-four hours.

2. Obligate yourself to follow up with your Booster in a couple of weeks to let them know what happened.

3. Set a reminder for two weeks to follow up with the Booster, regardless of whether you have connected with the new contact.

4. Initiate outreach to the referral immediately (or Reply All to any introductory email your Booster sends) and set a 7B reminder to follow up on the referral in case they do not respond.

5. Update the Booster when the two-week reminder triggers.

6. Enter a recurring monthly reminder in your calendar (the format of which we'll discuss in our final chapter) to keep your Booster updated on your progress.

It's not complex, but having a process for handling it makes it especially easy to manage.

So, what do I do in the nonjackpot scenario, when my interviewer asks me specifically what kind of resources I'm looking for?

You deflect the conversation toward nonreferral resources. The worst-case scenario at this point in the conversation is explicitly asking, "Who should I talk to next at your firm?" This implicitly violates your contention that you were interested in insights and advice rather than a job. Worse than that, however, is if your interviewer says, "Nobody comes to mind right now, but I'll let you know if I think of anyone." Ouch. Informational meeting dead end. Not even Boosters appreciate being put on the spot so directly.

I don't know about you, but I would never give a contact to a stranger without checking that it was okay with my contact first. Honestly, I find this situation so uncomfortable that, in the past, I have said, "Nobody comes to mind right now" even when I had someone in mind, simply because saying, "Let me check with my contact to see if it's okay if I hand you off to them" felt too uncomfortably transparent!

Boosters may want to offer you a contact but feel similarly protective of their network, given that they've known those people far longer than they've known you. If your contact doesn't offer you a referral contact immediately, don't ask for one—this gives you a second chance to ask for one later. Executing that second-chance request appropriately may even help you extract a referral from Obligates (once again leveraging the Ben Franklin effect), but we'll discuss how best to accomplish this at the end of this chapter.

So how do I respond if an interviewer asks me for clarification about what resources I'm seeking?

You deflect the questions toward resources of information and pointedly away from sources of advocacy (referrals). Here are some examples of good Resource questions:

- "Are there any annual conferences/industry websites/LinkedIn Groups pertaining to your work that you find particularly helpful?"

- "What's the most important ten minutes of research you do each week to stay current on your space?"

- "If you wanted to learn to speak like someone already in the industry prior to actually entering it, how would you go about doing that if you were me?"

These questions are far less threatening and are much lower risk than asking for referrals, particularly if you sense apprehension on the part of your contact. These questions are also durable—they can be used again and again, earning unique answers each time.

How can the answers I get from Resource questions be useful later?

The answers to these questions provide you with employee-approved ways for getting smarter about the sector and organization you are trying to join. This means that instead of being forced to rely on Google and Wikipedia to conduct your own external research, you can "use what the pros use," following the same techniques and reading the same news sources that your contacts themselves do to stay on top of their industries.

Thus, although you are not getting referrals (yet, at least), you are still collecting usable information that will help you in your future conversations.

Remember, these follow-up Resource questions can be cut for time in the jackpot scenario where you got a referral in response to asking the Pivot question. However, if time permits (and especially if you did not get a referral in response to the Pivot), move on to the final step of TIARA: Assignments.

ASSIGNMENT QUESTIONS

We have framed our contact as an expert and systematically converted a former stranger into a mentor over the course of our thirty-minute conversation. Assignment (aka project) questions are purely focused on gaining usable information rather than building rapport. Their goal is to help you speak the vernacular of the industry, gain an understanding of the high-value work under way right now, and develop an answer to the question, "We're not sure how we could use someone of your qualifications—what sort of work would you be able to do for us?"

This question is asked more frequently than you might imagine, especially at smaller organizations (remember that employers with two to ninety-nine employees account for nearly two-thirds of all US employment [see the table on page 18]). These smaller firms may not have a vacant position waiting for you, but if you can explain how the employer could improve their bottom line by bringing you on—even just by naming the projects they already know they need to get done—they may create a brand-new role for you.

Larger employers usually know where a job seeker with your skill and experience profile might fit in, but regardless of the employer's size, it is incumbent on you to be able to offer the organizations you approach some ideas about where you might fit in so they have something meaningful to react to beyond generic attributes like "problem solving" and "communication skills."

Here are some good Assignment questions:

- "Which project of yours do you feel has had the greatest impact?"

- "Has any particular type of project increased in popularity recently at your organization?"

- (If seeking internships or contract work) "Have you used interns or contractors in the past? If so, what sorts of projects have they done?"

How can the answers I get from Assignment questions be useful later?

The answers you get will help you build your mental toolbox of the types of projects that are increasingly in demand at your targeted employers. When a potential employer says, "We've never hired any-one with your background before—what sort of work could you do for us?" you should *not* respond, "I'll do anything you need me to." This demonstrates desperation rather than savvy, and it may result in you fetching coffee rather than doing any meaningful work.

Instead, invoke the "power of the first draft." It's much easier to critique someone else's ideas than it is to create your own from scratch, so relieve your potential employer of that burden by instead suggesting roles for yourself and engaging the employer in why or why not such a role may be feasible. This increases their likelihood of coming up with alternatives, which are far easier to brainstorm than entirely new ideas.

To invoke the power of the first draft, suggest to the employer some projects that you would be capable of doing that you think may create value for them, based on what you've learned from your other informationals. In my earlier example, I could take what I learned from my Kraft and General Mills informationals to a smaller consumer packaged goods company. When they say they aren't sure where a job seeker like me would fit into their company, it's far better for me to be specific and say, "I know fluctuating oil prices are driving your competitors to revamp their distribution strategies, so I could analyze your current structure to look for savings opportunities, for example."

I could add, "I could also do a customer segmentation analysis or a market size estimation for your next new product under launch consideration, or I could manage any packaging redesigns you have under way, as well." All of these projects may be ones the company already has in process or completed, but they demonstrate that I understand what actual work my targeted position entails. This in turn makes me a much more credible candidate than one who says, "I'll do whatever you need me to do" to a firm that has no idea how to use a person like me in the first place!

Furthermore, the assignments (aka projects) you identify during your informationals will help you identify connections back to the employer's needs when answering any Big Four questions you may receive in future informationals and job interviews. (See page 167 for a refresher).

Assignment questions can be cut for time if necessary or if you get a referral and it feels like the conversation is drawing to a close. But these questions can give you a nice jolt of legitimacy at the end of the conversation—before you enter Movement #3: Next Steps— because you're taking an active interest in the projects you'd likely be assigned if hired.

Shouldn't I ask what I can do for my contact?

This is another "sexy" piece of career advice that seems impossible to disagree with, but I'm going to anyway. The cons to me *far* outweigh the pros.

The pros of offering help to your potential Booster is that it does seem like basic manners—this person has helped you, so shouldn't you offer to help them? Most often they won't have any favors to request of you, so it's a costless gesture!

However, the cons of this approach are that it seems to ignore the science we learned in chapter 6: The 6-Point Email. Not only do you risk switching this person from social norms to market norms by mechanically attempting to repay a favor (by turning the relationship into a tit-for-tat series of transactions), you are also very unlikely to succeed at adequately doing so.

Instances where job seekers are able to immediately help people one to two levels above them are so rare that it strikes me as inauthentic and sales-y to offer. You are *not* this person's peer! Trying to repay their genuine gift of free consulting by putting them on the spot and asking them to immediately estimate the price of that advice in the form of a reciprocal request is a lot like offering them $5 to move a couch.

As the Ben Franklin effect states, when trying to deepen a relationship, it is more effective to acknowledge the magnitude of a favor than to attempt to immediately repay it. The single most realistic and authentic way to "repay" the favor is to find *and communicate back* the real value that their advice provided to you.

That doesn't happen overnight—putting their advice into practice and discovering its value takes time. We'll talk more about how to do this when we address following-up in chapter 10, but rest assured, your potential Boosters won't miss out—most mentors won't hesitate to ask their mentees for a favor if there is one they can identify that would be of true value.

Finally, if you feel you absolutely must offer your assistance, I'd invert the advice from the 6-Point Email by framing your offer as a statement rather than a question (as in "Please let me know if I can ever be of assistance" rather than "Is there anything I can do for you?"). This way you do not put your Booster on the spot or abruptly shift the conversation's tenor in an uncomfortable way right at the end.

What if I can *help my potential Booster?*

If a way you can help your potential Booster organically arose during the conversation, by all means offer that service (for example, send an article or website you referenced in conversation). However, don't force it. You will get better advocacy from someone who views you as a mentee than from someone who views you as a peer.

*Should my questions change if the person I'm speaking to is in
a junior role to the one I am pursuing?*

While you won't typically be doing informationals with people
junior to you, since the contacts you are targeting will tend to be
one to two levels above where you'd start, occasionally you will find
yourself doing an informational with a junior employee, usually
because you were referred to them or because you ran out of senior
people to reach out to.

In these cases, you may choose to cut Assignment questions, but
the rest of your TIARA questions will not change significantly. You
will still spend the first half of the conversation framing the person as
an expert and gradually converting them into a mentor. It is especially
flattering when a more senior person expresses an interest in a younger
one's insight, and these contacts will have viewpoints on both their
immediate sector and their firm in particular that are unknown to you.

For example, it may feel odd to ask a junior graphic designer
about the trends they are witnessing in their work when you may end
up becoming their boss (or boss's boss) eventually, but their perspective will help you better understand the challenges that organization
is facing and an appreciation for what is happening in the trenches
as well as at the five-hundred-foot level. Is the employer keeping up
with new technology? Do the junior team members juggle multiple
projects at once or handle them one at a time sequentially?

So, no, the Trends, Insights, and Resources questions will largely
stay the same in this situation, while the Advice questions will change
slightly in framing and tone (for example, "What best practices have
you seen among the managers you've had at the firm?").

The critical step is getting your contacts to empathize enough with
you to be willing to advocate for you in their organization—this comes
from trust rather than knowledge, so take the time to treat them as the
experts they are in their respective spaces and at their respective levels.
For all you know, it could be the first time in years that someone's asked
this person's opinion—and as Ben Franklin learned, simple recognition
of a person's knowledge is sometimes all it takes to create a lifelong ally.

That said, with Q&A complete, it's time to move on to our finale.

Movement #3: Next Steps

So how do I wrap up this conversation especially given that my goal is to get an interview?

Well, if we hit the jackpot and found a Booster who immediately volunteered to pass us on to a relevant colleague, we already know our next steps—we follow up with the referral we got from our contact and update the Booster in a couple of weeks on our progress (or lack thereof). We simply state those steps aloud, thank the Booster for spending time with us, and then send a quick thank-you email that night or the next day.

If we don't get a referral immediately during our informational meeting—and you should expect this to be the norm rather than the exception—you'll want to use what I call a Two-Part Informational Closing, where the first part (appreciation) happens a week before the second part (a direct request for a referral). This technique gives you a second chance to obtain referrals later, with a higher probability of success than if you put your contact on the spot and directly ask for referrals at this point. Two-Part Informational Closing sounds something like this:

> Our time is up, but thank you so much for your time today. You've given me a lot to think about.
>
> I'm going to take the weekend to reflect on all you've shared, but if I have any additional questions, is it okay if I reach back out to you?

It would be very difficult for even the most obdurate of Obligates to say no to a conditional request like this one. This requires no effort from your contact whatsoever—the next steps are entirely on you.

In psychologist Robert Cialdini's 1984 book *Influence: The Psychology of Persuasion*, he illustrates the power of getting a seemingly minimal and meaningless yes from a stranger, using a concept he calls "commitment and consistency." In one study he cites, an experimenter goes to a beach, lays a blanket a few feet away from another beachgoer (chosen at random), and settles in with a cooler and radio for some quality time in the sun. Shortly thereafter, the experimenter steps away to grab refreshments or go for a short walk.

A few minutes later, a second experimenter happens by and pretends to steal the first experimenter's radio. The experiment measured the bystander beachgoer's response to the "crime."

Depressingly, in only 20 percent of cases did the beachgoer intervene, yelling, "Stop, thief!" or attempting to track down the stolen goods. However, one simple change was introduced into the experiment that dramatically increased the intervention rate from 20 to 95 percent—care to take a guess what it was?

When I ask for guesses from the audiences I lecture to about 2HJS, the answers range from "pay the beachgoer to watch their stuff" to "hide the radio with their blanket" to "turn the radio off." In truth, all it takes to turn the detached bystander into a beach blanket vigilante is for the first experimenter to ask the test subject, "Would you mind watching my things?" before stepping away.[4]

Good manners make it nearly impossible to say no to small-probability requests like that one—turning that request down would usually require an elaborate story or an admission of imminent departure, as in, "I would, but I'm leaving in a few minutes myself." Barring that, though, an incredible 75 percent of test subjects (from 20 percent up to 95 percent) intervened only because they had verbally committed to watching the experimenter's things. The subject thus established (if only accidentally) a self-image as "someone who watches other people's things when asked," and the desire for consistency with that self-image (and the desire to minimize the cognitive dissonance inherent in breaking that promise) compelled the subject to action.

That is how you get Obligates who agreed to an informational meeting to help you. You leverage their fear of awkwardness, guilt, and bad manners to get them to make a tiny initial commitment, even if they don't really want to. Once they do that, however, they have further obligated themselves to be available in the future if you decide this is something you want to pursue (which it usually will be—it's a top target, after all!). To have their bases covered in case you do follow up, Obligates will likely do *just enough* legwork to give you something of value. This may simply be a few job postings they found internally or similar organizations to consider, but in some cases it's just easier for them to pass you on to a friendlier colleague or the actual hiring manager than to come up with a cover story for why they had to renege on their promise to help you.

Thankfully, Boosters don't need any formal psychological technique in order to be motivated to help you. However, Obligates can actually become equally productive contacts themselves through your proper execution of the "commitment and consistency" concept—eventually, their self-image will grow to include, "I'm the type of person who lives up to my commitments to assist job seekers I've promised to help."

Go into every informational meeting assuming you'll need to use a Two-Part Informational Closing—with follow-up required to get a useful contact. If you gauchely ask for a contact during an initial informational and fail to get one, you've hit a dead end with that contact—it's awful to lose a Booster simply because you put the person on the spot.

By ending the conversation with the Two-Part Informational Closing just described, you're allowing several positive developments the chance to occur offline. First, this delay gives your contacts a breather during which they can decide whether they like and trust you enough to pass you on to a colleague. Second, it demonstrates that the promise you made in your email was sincere—the entirety of your conversation was about gathering insight and advice, and not about getting a job, and your thank-you note similarly did not involve an upsell. Third, it allows your contact the space and time offline to identify and touch base with their referral to see whether that person is open to speaking with you.

Finally, and most important, this technique allows you to *maintain control of the follow-up process*. Using the Two-Part Informational

Closing, you are keeping your foot in the door so you have a second (and better) chance to get a referral from your contact a few days later even if the contact wasn't ready to offer one when you first spoke.

How do I conduct part two of the Two-Part Informational Closing, then?

First, be sure to send a thank-you note for the initial informational interview the day after the conversation—this goes both for informationals in which you get a contact as well as for those in which you don't. Again, this is just good form.

However, when you know a part two will be necessary, set yourself a reminder for the following business week (meaning a weekend has passed in between) to follow up with your contact—again, the reminder allows you to forget about the conversation until it is time to act, minimizing your stress.

If the contact has given you any advice that you can implement immediately—like starting to read *Brandweek* or *Ad Age* if you want to get familiar with marketing terminology—then certainly do so. Mentioning such immediate incorporation of advice in part two increases your credibility by demonstrating you're the type who follows the advice you're given, which, in turn, increases your contact's willingness to further invest in your welfare.

Now, to actually execute part two of the Two-Part Informational Closing, email your contact when your reminder pops up the following week and ask them explicitly for a referral while framing *them* as the hero in your story:

> *Thanks again for your time last week. Upon further reflection, this is definitely something I'd like to pursue further. How would you go about doing that if you were me? For example, can you recommend someone I should speak to next?*

Not all contacts are created equal, unfortunately, but you might be surprised at how even Obligates will come through for you from time to time when managed in such commitment-and-consistency–oriented fashion.

If you do get a referral during this follow-up inquiry, thank your contact for their time and guidance and, just like in the "jackpot scenario," promise to update them in a couple of weeks with the results of their assistance to you. If you don't get a contact or any helpful information from this follow-up, this contact is likely a dead end, indicating that you've hooked an Obligate at your target organization. You will still set a recurring monthly reminder to check in with this person and update them of your progress, since this apparent Obligate gave you the gift of their time and (albeit rarely) may warm to you over time and offer you more assertive assistance in the future. However, we can't rely on any further assistance from them, so you will also immediately start up the 3B7 Routine with a brand-new contact until you're confident you've found someone who truly wants to see you succeed sooner rather than later and gives you concrete rather than vague advice.

Not every informational meeting yields results—that is why it is especially important to have a process whereby you prioritize your target employers (your LAMP list) before initiating a process (the 3B7 Routine) for systematically requesting, scheduling, and conducting informationals with your highest-priority targets simultaneously.

When you job-seek in this fashion, no single fruitless informational interview is a failure—it's simply an investment that hasn't paid off yet. As my dear mother used to say, "The difference between a good meal and a bad meal is about an hour"—that is to say, you might be a great fit but are simply in the right place at the wrong time. Thus, in the next chapter, we'll discuss how to maximize our follow-up to achieve the best possible results from the informationals we *do* conduct, using a process called the Harvest Cycle.

TROUBLESHOOTING

What if my contact starts our conversation by saying, "I'm very busy and only have a few minutes to talk, so just tell me how I can help you"?

This is classic Obligate behavior. The problem is that you have no idea whether the person truly is a Booster who suddenly became busy but still really wants to help or an Obligate who wants this to be over as soon as possible!

Therefore, offer to postpone the conversation until the contact has more time. If they gratefully accept (and you two can agree on a date within the next week or so to speak), you've likely found a Booster. You've also demonstrated excellent emotional intelligence by how you handled the situation, putting the contact's needs before yours. The contact now "owes you one," and you are continuing to build your track record of fulfilling your commitments and taking stress out of the contact's life.

If your contact resists rescheduling the conversation and insists on doing an abbreviated conversation at that moment, that's a trickier situation. Obligates will be very open to postponing but very resistant to rescheduling, because it implies the conversation will be longer later than it would be now, and their "obligation" will hang over them even longer than it already has. That said, Boosters do also occasionally respond this way, recognizing that speed trumps conversation duration if open positions are currently available.

In either case, if the contact insists on having the conversation right then, I'd advise you to immediately jump to the "Advice" section of the TIARA Framework (with a dash of Insight questions thrown in), with a question like, "Given what you've learned in your time at your employer, what would you do, if you were me, to maximize your chances?" You are requesting insight, empathy, and creativity all at once—it's basically a one-question version of TIARA.

How your contact responds to this will be telling. If they resist engagement, speaking generally and in the second person with a response like, "Just keep talking to people

continued

TROUBLESHOOTING

here, and eventually something will turn up," you've probably found yourself an Obligate, the job search equivalent of landing an old shoe while out fishing. Hey, it happens. It's a cost of doing business, and not every raffle ticket will be a winner.

However, if the contact speaks more specifically—for example, "If I were you, I would reach out to Tim Choi—I think he's still looking for someone right now, but if he isn't, he would likely know who is . . ."—it's likely you've found a busy Booster who genuinely wants to help but simply needs to do so quickly, given their other commitments.

If the earlier question isn't your style, you can skip the integration of Insight and go straight for the job search jugular with a pure Advice question. I suggest asking, "What do you know now that you wish you knew when you were in my position as a job seeker trying to break into this space/organization?" The nature of their response will still fall into either the Booster or the Obligate camp.

If the person resists giving you any real advice, you've found an Obligate and need to keep following the 3B7 Routine to find a Booster. However, if you do get a real lead, then assume the person is a Booster and pursue that recommended avenue as if you had conducted a full-length informational with the Booster; that is, obligate yourself to follow up in a couple of weeks with the results of the proffered help.

In short, the easiest way to tell an Obligate from a Booster (and this can be difficult to do when you're just starting out) is by the specificity of their guidance; *Boosters tend to give you concrete guidance, while Obligates tend to stay vague.*

However, if the referral does not respond and your Booster doesn't offer to assist you further (or respond at all) when you report your lack of results, the presumed Booster was probably just an Obligate seeking to "pass the buck" to a colleague. Again, no worries—it's part of the process.

TROUBLESHOOTING

In general, when a contact tries to rush through an informational interview, it's a bad sign—most likely you've found an Obligate.

What if my contact asks me to submit the questions I'd like to ask over email?

This is a common variation of our first Troubleshooting question. It is unclear whether this is a Booster who wants to help but prefers email (and/or wants to ensure in advance you're not going to ask for a job) or an Obligate who is looking to minimize their effort and relationship building with you. In general, I'd assume the latter, but that doesn't mean you can't get useful information here, even from Obligates.

Again, similar to the previous question, I'd attempt a condensed TIARA informational in no more than three questions. The first question I'd offer would be a Trend question to prime creativity and portray them as an expert while also giving them a fun and flattering question to warm up with. (Furthermore, they may realize that your questions can be answered faster in real time than over email.) For example, I might pick, "In your opinion, what macro trend is most impacting your space right now?" You could also pick an Insight question here, but given those are a little more intimate and this person is a perfect stranger, doing so may come off as a bit intrusive.

The second question I'd offer would be an Advice question, where I'd frame my contact as the protagonist in my search; like, "If you were me, what would you be doing right now to best prepare for a career in this field?" (or if you have relevant experience already, "What do you know now that you wish you knew when you were in my position trying to break into this organization?"). This shifts your focus to portray them as a mentor while directly asking them for empathy for your situation.

continued

The third question I'd offer would be a variation of the Pivot itself: "What resource(s) would you recommend I look into next to maximize my chance of identifying whether there might be a mutual fit?" This is indeed a bit more of a direct formulation than the mid-informational Pivot, but you don't have much to lose in this situation, since it already does not look promising that the contact will have a real-time chat with you. Furthermore, if this person is indeed an Obligate, they are motivated by a sense of obligation, so by framing your interest as a desire to learn more about whether there's a mutual fit (rather than asking for an interview directly), you may still tap into a begrudging referral to HR; and even a blind (no-conversation) referral to HR from an Obligate may be enough to get you a screening interview—with minimal effort, no less!

All that having been said, keep your expectations low here given it really seems to take real-time interaction with another person to acquire true advocacy; and don't hesitate to resume 3B7 and contact a new person at that same organization if you don't get an email reply within three business days.

What if my contact cancels our conversation at the last minute?

Try to reschedule the conversation to the best of your ability, but recognize if rescheduling proves difficult, this is very typical Obligate behavior. By doing this, Obligates are hoping, consciously or subconsciously, that if they treat you poorly enough, you'll go away. Simply grant Obligates their wish in this case and move on; resume 3B7 with new contacts until you find someone who's genuinely interested in your welfare.

TROUBLESHOOTING

What if a contact agrees to speak with me but warns me in advance that the employer is not hiring right now?

Take that call! If the person was an Obligate, they'd do whatever they could to avoid actually scheduling this conversation with you. However, if the person is happy and excited to talk to you anyway, you may have found a Super-Booster.

Informationals with firms that aren't hiring are great for several reasons. First, there's no pressure. Second, if you leave a good impression, you're at the top of the contact's list when the employer does start hiring again, because you demonstrated a genuine interest even when told jobs were off the table. Third, and most important, Boosters at a nonhiring firm have the potential to help you with multiple firms rather than just their own!

Remember Adam's story from chapter 1 (pages 27-28)? An IT consultant who wanted to get into the mobile phone industry, he found a job with the mobile industry's standards board because he conducted informationals with employers who told him in advance they couldn't hire him. Adam used those conversations to build his knowledge of the industry and the credibility of his interest, and when it came time for the Pivot question in TIARA, he had license to directly ask his interviewer, "What other organizations should I make sure I have on my radar right now, given my job search goals?" and "Which firms in this space are doing exciting things right now?"

His Booster couldn't help him with their own employer, but they did offer him contacts at several less obvious, smaller organizations that, thanks to their lower profiles, weren't being inundated by interested candidates.

Boosters *want* to help you. When their own employers are not an option, Boosters are liberated to connect you to employers elsewhere (and you are similarly liberated to ask about other employers), which can lead to internal

continued

referrals at several firms rather than just one. Instead of treating this situation as a dead end, treat it as a risk-free chance to find out which organizations are on the rise.

What if a hiring manager tells me I'm simply not a fit for their firm?

Most employers would not be so direct. They prefer more ambiguous language like, "We'll keep your name on file, and we'll reach out to you if we identify a potential fit." But a rose by any other name smells as sweet, so assume "we'll keep your name on file" means "no."

Regardless, this is why we have a LAMP list. When we have a Booster who gives us a specific timeline (for example, "Check back with me in mid-April—that's when we start identifying projects"), set yourself a reminder to reconnect with that employer then. After that, move on to the next new employer on your LAMP list. Conversely, when an employer tells you employment is not an option—for whatever reason—simply open your LAMP list, delete that employer's row of data (do *not* mark it in red or otherwise leave it visible—that will make the relevant employers in your list harder to find and constantly remind you of a setback, which serves no practical purpose), and send your first outreach email to the next target on your list. No thinking, just execution.

Rejection stings momentarily, as it should—this is what compels you to reevaluate your previous efforts, seek feedback, and innovate. That's growth—an ability universally appreciated by employers. It's also a call to action. You have too many other targets to be wasting time on one with bad taste in potential employees!

## CHAPTER 10

FOLLOW-UP

So I just conducted an informational meeting—now what?

The benefits of informational meetings rarely reveal themselves immediately. The goal of this chapter is to help you extract the maximum benefit from each contact you do speak with in a systematic and efficient fashion—using a process I call the *Harvest Cycle*. As with farming, all the groundwork you've done planting seeds up until this point is meaningless if you're not prepared to harvest the results. I've seen too many job seekers do the hard work of creating LAMP lists, finding contacts, drafting and tracking outreach, and preparing for and conducting informationals only to fail to do what is perhaps both the easiest yet most important aspect of the job search: following up. That is why the Harvest Cycle was created for this revised edition of 2HJS.

Many job seekers who are new to job searching, particularly away from the confines of a university's career center, expect informational interviewing to be like fishing for fish. You bait the hook, toss the line in the water, a fish swims up and grabs it, and there's your dinner (or it doesn't, and you try again tomorrow).

Unfortunately, it's actually a lot more like fishing for lobsters. Lobsters don't swim up to baited hooks. Instead, you need to set traps for them in the ocean, which you check on every day or two to see whether any lobsters were caught. That is the most maddening aspect of the job search—there is zero instant gratification.

My Fuqua students face a major challenge with this arrangement—not only because engaging in social activities does provide immediate rewards, but also because even schoolwork provides a more predictable reward than the job search does. You spend an extra hour studying for a statistics quiz, you get an hour's worth of a better grade later. In contrast, if you spend thirty minutes conducting an informational meeting, it can take weeks or even months before you know whether that effort results in an interview. You also never know which meeting is going to be the one that leads to a job!

Because the job search offers such uncertainty and long-delayed rewards, committing to a structured approach like the Harvest Cycle is critical—otherwise, it becomes far too easy to avoid or abandon a job search before your efforts have a chance to yield their full returns.

Many students consider finding a better job the primary reason for going (back) to school in the first place. Similarly, most unhappily employed job seekers consider finding a better job to be the fastest route to a happier life. If you've read this far, you're obviously open to learning a new approach and investing effort in order to change your situation but recognize that a systematic follow-up process is just as important as a systematic outreach process.

So how do I systematize my follow-up?

Anytime you complete *any* informational meeting, send a thank-you email that evening or the next day. (Emails reach your contact faster and are easier to archive than hard-copy thank-you notes. For more on this, see Time Out #7.) This person did you a favor, so regardless of the outcome, they've earned your thanks.

Thanks, but No Thanks

I must get asked monthly about handwritten thank-you notes, mostly because a job seeker was told by someone—be it a career columnist, a coach, or a parent—that this was critical to do. I would agree if emailing thank-you notes was not an option, sure. However, emailed thank-you notes are superior in several ways. They're not only faster and easier to store for later reference, but they're also free and don't require time and effort (to procure stationery, postage, and mailing addresses).

More generally, my rule of thumb for any "extra" efforts in the job search is this: if the downsides are certain but the upsides are uncertain, don't do it. I'd put handwritten thank-you notes firmly in this category.

For handwritten thank-you notes to be worth the effort, they'd have to regularly lead to referrals that you would *not* have gotten from an emailed thank-you note alone. There's just no proof that this happens. There's no proof that it *doesn't* happen either, but that's exactly why I created my rule of thumb; if you don't know for sure, save your energy.

That said, if you're passionate about this, and cranking out handwritten thank-you notes feels intuitive rather than arduous, you absolutely do you. Just send a thank-you note by email as well in case your note of appreciation does not arrive by the time you ask for your referral in a week!

Full disclosure, though? I do wish this particular piece of advice would die in a courteous yet classy fire.

In addition, if the contact offered you a referral immediately, you would have obligated yourself (in your thank-you note, if not in the conversation itself) to provide an update on your progress in a couple of weeks.

Beyond that, you will want to set up a recurring one-month reminder in your calendar after each informational interview. Your Boosters may not know how to help you at the moment of your first conversation, but if you've left a good impression, they will start hearing things about potential job openings that they had previously ignored. I call this *subsequent relevance*.

Given your Boosters already have jobs, they've been ignoring information about jobs at your level, just as we ignore banner ads on websites we frequently check for news, weather, or sports scores. However, once our Boosters know we exist, this information *subsequently becomes relevant* (just as we notice banner ads when they advertise products we just looked up on Amazon). However, they may not connect the dots and proactively notify you when they hear mention of a relevant opening; instead, they'll typically remember just enough to direct you to it the next time you check in.

Thus, once you give Boosters a reason to care, they effectively become an extra set of ears for you. By checking back in monthly, you accomplish several goals: you remind them you're still job-seeking, you renew your interest in their firm specifically, and you give them a prompt to take action (because we all know clicking Reply, for whatever odd-but-true reason, is infinitely easier than clicking New Email . . .). Furthermore, these check-ins don't require another phone call nor any substantive requests on your part—it's truly the thought (and reminder) that counts.

So, what should these monthly check-in emails consist of, exactly?

These emails start off simple, and they get even simpler over time! Also—like everything else in this process—they follow a pretty basic pattern. The first check-in, in particular, is quite formulaic yet very effective.

The basic structure of this check-in is as follows:

1. Recap of advice given in previous conversation

2. Summary of specific benefits derived from following that advice

3. Request for any further suggestions they might have

In practice, a check-in email (which, to be clear, would be sent a month after either (a) you attempted part two of a Two-Part Informational Closing but did not get a referral or (b) you reported the results of a referral you did receive to your Booster) could look like this:

Subject: Ad Age / Brand Week & update

Hi Jerry,

I wanted to send you a quick update. I found the insights you shared last month incredibly helpful, especially those on the increasing role of microsegmentation in the advertising space. Per your advice, I also started reading *Brand Week* and *Ad Age*, and I'm already feeling much more confident in my ability to discuss trends impacting ad agencies today.

Might you have any additional suggestions? Your insights are greatly appreciated, and I'll certainly keep you posted of my progress.

Sincerely,

Ari

The first update email will be the longest one, as you have to refer to your notes from your prior conversation, reiterate any advice they may have given you, and describe your follow-through. If you receive additional advice in response to this update email, repeat the process next month.

However, if your contact does not have new advice for you, simply make your subsequent monthly check-ins more personal in nature, like this:

Subject: Checking in & update

Hi Anthony,

How are you? And how is your little one doing? Congratulations again to you and Kimberly on becoming new parents.

On my end, my networking conversations are continuing. Your insights have been invaluable, though. I've had some traction with a few of the agencies you suggested, and I'm about to interview with one later this week.

Thanks again for your mentorship in this process, and I hope to have some good news to share with you in the near future!

Yours truly,

Ari

These monthly check-ins may not seem like much. Again, they are rather formulaic and your ask is minimal—merely requesting a brief personal update. However, they are the equivalent of periodically checking your lobster traps for a catch.

Believe it or not, you are providing your Boosters with a service by sending these emails—a reminder to act if they've heard anything that might be relevant to you so they don't have to initiate that outreach themselves. Remember, Boosters want to help you, and even Obligates may forward you an internal posting if you make it easy enough (meaning you make it so easy that they simply can't justify not helping!).

Even better, these updates will not be perceived as extra work or pushy by your Boosters. Recall, Boosters by definition are predisposed to be actively helpful. Plus, they have never known you in any other context than an actively job-seeking one, so your regular check-ins will feel responsible rather than jarringly urgent. This is precisely why trying to get an existing contact who has known you in non-job-seeking contexts (such as a college friend or acquaintance you met at a conference a year or two ago) is so difficult—the tonal shift and newfound prioritization you're asserting is often too far a bridge to cross from the status quo.

A month may not seem like a long time to wait between messages before you start 2HJS, but once you realize how fast things start moving when you launch 3B7 (which gets progressively busier with each passing week), you will realize it is plenty of time to wait between updates. However, if you wait a few months to check back in with a Booster, their sense of urgency around your search is likely to have dissipated and you will have to start over again with new contacts.

When executed exactly as laid out in this book, most 2HJS-based searches take a month or two (and occasionally longer for more experienced professionals, simply because fewer jobs exist at senior levels than junior), so you will not need to worry about doing months and months of check-in emails. You'll usually only get through one or maybe two before you land. That is, again, assuming you follow the steps as written!

Again, although many of the steps of 2HJS are approximate as with cooking, the follow-up in the Harvest Cycle (just like 3B7) is precise, as with baking. If you don't keep your Boosters regularly updated, you risk losing the urgency of that relationship. That urgency absolutely will go away once you find employment, but until that point, you need to keep them in the loop and ensure their engagement. Doing so only requires one email a month, but as you get deeper into this process, you will have more Boosters to update monthly, each one an additional set of eyes and ears watching for openings on your behalf.

What if my contact doesn't respond to my check-in email at all?

If you receive no response, simply wait until the next month's reminder to follow up. Then be sure to frame your check-in email as a question (ending in a question mark) rather than a statement (ending in a period) so your contact knows a response is expected either way, their response in turn reassures you that they are still engaging with you and, presumably, on your behalf as well. If you do not get a response at that point or you doubt their current engagement, begin outreach to a new contact.

I *think* I've got it, but isn't a picture supposed to be worth a thousand words?

Indeed, now is the perfect time to show you the entire Harvest Cycle process, covering the end of the informational to the post-meeting follow-up period, plotted out in flow chart form. Note that gray boxes denote action steps:

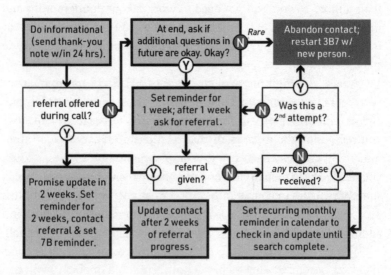

So will all these monthly follow-ups become burdensome as I work my way down my LAMP list?

As your network of advocates grows, you will indeed spend more time harvesting—checking back in and following up with your Boosters—than you did initially. But these follow-ups can always be done by email, and you won't be sending more than one or two per contact given most 2HJS-based searches are done within a few months. It truly is more the thought (or more specifically, the reminder) that counts. The time that each follow-up takes will be minimal—you'll just be doing it more often since the further in the process you get, the more Boosters you will have to check in with.

In the meantime, once you feel you've identified a true Booster at a Top 5 target on your LAMP list, you now have bandwidth to network with a new employer, so initiate outreach to the next employer on your LAMP list. The process doesn't get more complicated or harder as you go along—you simply repeat Parts 2 and 3 (Contact and Convince) of 2HJS until you land an offer. It's repetitive but not difficult.

Using *The 2-Hour Job Search*, your probability of success grows with each new relationship formed and Booster identified. Eventually, your network will grow so wide that you'll be offered job interviews with relative regularity due to the ever-growing advocacy network you've created.

Lest you think this process is an infinite loop, rest assured that in practice, none of my job seekers who've adopted this process (*exactly*, mind you) have gotten much further than number ten on their LAMP lists before something panned out. (That said, if I had a dime for every time someone's told me they've "gotten all the way through their LAMP list" without success, only to find they took great liberties along the way—for example, emailing every employer on their list exactly once before moving on, or defining "getting all the way through their LAMP list" as having applied online to every employer on their list—I would have several dollars' worth of frustratingly earned dimes.)

For my conscientious 2HJS adherents, it wasn't just their adoption of a systematic approach that got them hired, though. With that systematic approach came a newfound confidence, one that was visible in their interviews. They knew there were dozens of other fish (employers) in the sea, and recruiters always find candidates who project that particular brand of nonchalant confidence more desirable than others.

It's perfectly rational behavior, in fact. Employers can safely assume that how you approach your job search is how you'll approach the job. Organizations don't want job seekers who treat hope as a strategy, mainly because *hope is not a strategy*. Organizations want employees who create plans of action, complete with backup plans for when things inevitably go wrong. Candidates who clearly have other lines in the water are more likely to be that kind of employee.

Be *that* kind of candidate.

TROUBLESHOOTING

What if I'm not able to start working for many months? When should I start my search?

Whether you are available immediately or not until graduation many months from now, start your search as soon as you are ready to fully commit to the 2HJS process, recognizing that earlier is always better than later—but 100 percent several months from now is better than 80 percent right now (once again, the Harvest Cycle, like 3B7, is more like baking than cooking).

Note that you never explicitly ask for a job in 2HJS; therefore, you can start looking as soon as you're ready, and if a Top 5 organization offers you an interview for a role they need to fill before you'd be able to start working, you can politely decline and thank them for their interest, secure in the knowledge that you're now on their "call list," and you'll therefore be contacted for subsequent openings as well.

Starting your networking early offers several key benefits:

- For career changers, it provides a great way to test your assumptions about how good a fit one or more career paths will be, which then provides you with

TROUBLESHOOTING

more time to iterate and pivot if you discover that one
or more of your targeted career paths is a bad match.

- For students targeting just-in-time sectors (like tech
start-ups), networking in the fall for positions that
typically start recruiting in the spring or summer differ-
entiates you from job seekers who tend to use
just-in-time sectors as backups to sectors that hire many
months in advance (like consulting, banking, big tech,
and other industries populated by very large employers).

- For *everyone*, starting early allows you to lean into
learning, enabling you to take your time and have your
set of Boosters identified well in advance of when you're
actually able to interview. This allows you a better
chance of getting *all* your options on the table before
having to make a decision.

Part 3: Convince Wrap-Up

There are a number of different outcomes for each informational
meeting, but they fall more or less into three categories: **Advance**,
Hold, and **Drop**. Advances are when your contacts (either immediately
or after a scheduled follow-up) connect you directly to a hiring manager or ask you to send them a resume that they can pass along. This
is the ideal outcome, and if the job is indeed available, the Advance
usually leads to an interview in a matter of weeks. As always, you'll
promise to update your contacts with the results of their Advance in
a couple of weeks, so you can use that update as a way to check your
status for that particular opening.

It's a Hold when a contact responds to your follow-up outreach but
doesn't have any further helpful information at the current moment.
It is the empty lobster cage—no catches today, but that doesn't mean it
won't have dinner inside waiting for you tomorrow. You're effectively in
a holding pattern with these contacts, so focus your efforts elsewhere
until it's time to check in with them again.

continued

It's a Drop when a contact stops responding to your follow-up inquiries. Again, this is why I like to include in my follow-up emails at least one question, either personal or professional (for example, "How did that product launch project turn out for you?" or "Did you travel for the holidays?")—something that prompts your contact to give you a brief, simple response to show they're still engaged. Two consecutive check-ins without a response suggests a disengaged Obligate rather than a committed Booster, so start over with a new contact as the Harvest Cycle diagram suggests.

Employers are trying to compress the amount of time they spend on hiring—it isn't "productive" work (in that it won't help them get promoted), so the process now moves faster than it ever has before. This plays to your advantage if you follow 2HJS, because employers will start with the applicants they know and like before reviewing resumes of strangers.

It bears repeating: employers today vastly prefer finding "good enough" candidates quickly rather than "perfect" candidates slowly! "Good enough" candidates are usually found through personal connections and internal referrals—very rarely are they found by their CV alone. Therefore, the general rule of thumb I suggest is to *never* send a resume to anyone unless it has been asked for. An unsolicited resume is unlikely to be read and makes you look desperate.

With this approach, when your CV *does* get asked for, you know it is likely to get reviewed and/or forwarded, giving you information you didn't have before about that contact's willingness to help you and the employer's potential interest in your candidacy. An employer won't hire you without seeing your resume, but just because you send your resume doesn't mean it will be seen.

The follow-up process doesn't fundamentally change even if the contact does ask for your CV—you'll still offer to check back in two weeks to provide an update. However, you'll also keep repeating the process with other targets simultaneously—outreach, informational, follow-up—until a job offer is received. Initially, this process may seem scary, but you'll get used to it. Eventually, it will become as routine as brushing your teeth or watching your favorite movie for the hundredth time, but unlike those activities, each new iteration of *The 2-Hour Job Search* offers the potential to fundamentally change your life for the better!

CONCLUSION

It's counterintuitive, but right now is a great time to be looking for a job. The advent of online job postings has fundamentally changed how hiring gets done. People flocked to the concept due to its convenience. However, in practice, online job postings have proved to be nothing more than a massive red herring.

Submitting resumes online lets job seekers *feel* like they're looking for a job (i.e., the Defensive Job Search), so job seekers continue to use them, knowing full well how unlikely a response is. It's like watching someone beating up a vending machine for an hour, completely unwilling to accept that it just ate their money. Unfortunately, whoever invented the online job posting didn't invent a way to effectively screen out unqualified or mediocre candidates.

2HJS doesn't offer the same instant gratification that filling out online job postings does—it involves change, and its rewards (while far larger) are slower to arrive. Unlike online job postings, however, it does predictably work.

What makes right now such a great time to be looking is that, using 2HJS (either wholesale or cafeteria style for the parts you struggle with most), you are being strategic while others are flailing.

Dick Fosbury wasn't necessarily the best high jumper in the world in 1968. He actually struggled at the sport in high school, finding himself unable to use the traditional downward-facing "straddle method" due to a back deformity. Out of desperation, he resorted to an out-of-fashion technique called the upright scissors method, which he could perform—at least well enough to make his high school track team.

However, from this basic technique, he found his results improved as he leaned back during his jumps. Gradually, he modified this style even further so that he started going over the bar backward, headfirst, and face-up—thus, the "Fosbury Flop" was born.

He was the only person at the 1968 Olympics to use that method, and he won the gold medal, breaking the world record in the process. In the next Olympics in 1972, twenty-eight out of forty high jumpers had adopted the Fosbury Flop technique, and today every elite high jumper uses it.[1]

He cleared the highest bar that day in Mexico City, but Dick Fosbury may *not* have been the best high jumper in the world—just the best equipped. He had simply evolved beyond the rest of the field—his new "technology" (even with his limited coordination) trumped his competitors' superior natural abilities.

It's frustrating to know that jobs don't go to the most "qualified" candidates these days, just as it must have been infuriating for Dick Fosbury's opponents to experience defeat at the hands of such an unorthodox approach. However, the job search has never been fair. Are CVs mailed in on nice paper really a fairer way to select whom to interview than choosing only from a pool of internal referrals? Viewing the job search through the lens of "fairness" can drive you mad. It simply is what it is.

By reading this book, you have learned a process by which you can exploit the new rules of the job search. These rules are not a fad, either—even if the economy reached new heights tomorrow, there would still be no going back to the pre-internet job search days.

Technology—specifically, the online job posting—has broken the traditional job search. Luckily, it broke the job search *for everyone*—in that sense, it's actually a more "fair" time to job search now than ever before. The job search is experiencing its own Gold Rush era in which those who figure out how to find and collect the gold first get rich, while the rest struggle to keep up. The stakes are real here, but the path forward relies more on working smarter than working harder.

So learn the new job search board game and play it well, since jobs today are going to those who adapt most quickly and effectively to these new job search rules. My goal in writing *The 2-Hour Job Search* was to tell you exactly how to do that. The great news is that you can have a less impressive background than other candidates but still get a job with the right strategy. David *can* slay Goliath, but not without a slingshot.

On the flip side, remember that if you get complacent, you too can get Fosbury Flopped by inferior candidates who implement this method before you do. Superior qualifications used to speak for themselves, but the world is far too noisy for that now. If you've long been a Goliath in your industry, and you've suddenly found yourself in the job search, let this book help you reboot your career.

With this book, I wanted to demonstrate that the job search—while tedious at times—is utterly accomplishable. Even so, some of you may now be looking back and thinking this change in approach seems insurmountable. Perhaps you're not comfortable with spreadsheets, or informational meetings still seem too socially awkward to even attempt. Please resist that urge. Everyone is bad at an activity before they are good at it, and the job search is no different.

In her 2006 book *Mindset*, Stanford psychology professor Carol Dweck identified a concept called the *growth mindset* that is particularly relevant to the still skeptical among you. Fixed-mindset individuals tend to think that talents are largely static and strongly tied to one's natural abilities, while those with growth mindsets think that talents are like muscles—they can be developed over time with practice and effort, just as muscles can be stretched and microscopically torn so they grow stronger than before.

Interestingly, those with growth mindsets have been shown to adapt to change more effectively, cope better with failure, and even progress further in their careers. Even more interesting, the growth mindset can be *learned*.

The beauty of 2HJS is that it is largely repetitive once the basics are established. After the first few 3B7 Routine iterations and informational meetings, you'll be mastering these techniques the way twelve-year-olds master a new video game a week after their birthday.

I've watched the ambiguity and hopelessness of the job search bring adults to tears and rip families apart. It's truly awful. I hope this book has shown you it doesn't have to be that way. The job search will *always* be frustrating at times, sure, but it should never be overwhelming.

There's one last helpful concept I'd like to highlight from Chip and Dan Heath's fine book *Switch*, mentioned in chapter 2. The authors stress that "shrinking the change"—or viewing large problems as a series of smaller tasks—is critical to adopting a totally new approach to solving a problem.[3] In this book, we've done exactly that—shrunk the change by turning the job search into three discrete parts: Prioritize, Contact, and Convince.

In Part 1: Prioritize, we learned how to build a list of forty possible employers in forty minutes, using four different methods requiring just ten minutes apiece. We then collected three pieces of data that approximated the likelihood of success for each one. This gave us two resources: a large universe of possibilities and a precise order in which to pursue them, all in just over an hour.

In Part 2: Contact, we learned that less is more. Shorter outreach emails—particularly the kind created using the 6-Point Email process—are not only easier and faster to write, but they also maximize the probability of getting a response from Boosters (that is, the *right* kind of contacts) while helping to screen out Obligates and Curmudgeons. We also learned an airtight tracking system in the 3B7 Routine so that we could strategically ignore any to-dos that didn't require action on a particular day, leaving us more mental bandwidth to focus on time-sensitive tasks.

Finally, in Part 3: Convince, we learned a process for managing informational meetings to maximize the chances of meeting our dual goals: building rapport and gaining usable information. We learned which kinds of research were most critical to do in advance, how to initiate small talk, and how to systematically lead the conversation to earn that contact's advocacy. Finally, we learned how to follow up with those advocates systematically using the Harvest Cycle so minimal thought would be required but potentially great benefit could be extracted.

Even shrinking the change doesn't make job searching *fun*, but it will improve your quality of life, in terms of both your outcomes and your peace of mind during the process. I hope that, at a minimum, reading this book has removed most of the guesswork and confusion from the job search for you. You will still no doubt experience setbacks and curveballs along the way. I've tried to prepare you for the most common ones, but the new ones you encounter (which I hope you will share with me in "The 2-Hour Job Search—Q&A Forum" LinkedIn Group!) represent the insight portion of this process, bridging initial hope to eventual confidence. That's where innovation happens—and when *The 2-Hour Job Search* becomes your own.

QUICK-START GUIDE

This guide is not a substitute for reading the rest of the book. However, it should refresh your memory enough to help you execute the steps we covered earlier without having to flip back and forth.

Here's what we learned.

Part 1: Prioritize (the LAMP List)

1. List column (40 minutes total—4 methods × 10 minutes; 40-employer minimum in total)

    A. Dream employer method

        i. Type any "dream employers" that come to mind into the L column of your spreadsheet.

        ii. Determine common traits shared by your initial dream employers and use a search engine to identify employers who meet those and similar criteria.

    B. Alumni (or affinity) employer method

        i. Search alumni or affinity databases to find organizations where people like you hold interesting job titles in interesting locations.

    C. Actively hiring employer method

        i. Search Indeed.com (or similar) for organizations with currently available job postings of interest to you.

D. Trending employer method (if work authorized; visa employer method if not)

    i. Trending employer method: Read or Google trends in industries or functions of interest (e.g., "mobile gaming trends") for employer ideas.

    ii. Visa employer method: Use Visa database (e.g., Myvisajobs.com) to identify employers who recently sponsored people targeting your desired career path.

2. Advocacy column (10 minutes)

A. Search LinkedIn for advocates (for example, alumni from your most recent educational institution) at each employer in the L column.

B. Note only "Y" for "yes" and "N" for "no" in the Advocacy column—do not count or copy contact information.

3. Motivation column (5 minutes)

A. Assign target employers in the L column a qualitative score of 0 to 3, assessing your level of interest to approach each:

    i. Award a score of 3 to targets you find most motivating ("dream employers").

    ii. Award a score of 1 to targets you find least motivating *and with which you are familiar.*

    iii. Award a score of 0 to targets with which you are completely unfamiliar.

4. Posting column (15 minutes)

   A. Using Indeed.com or similar, classify current hiring activity on a 1 to 3 scale:

      i. Award a score of 3 when postings found are "very relevant."

      ii. Award a score of 2 when postings found are "somewhat relevant."

      iii. Award a score of 1 when no relevant postings are found.

5. LAMP List Wrap-up

   A. Sort your LAMP list priorities in this order:

      i. Motivation (largest to smallest)

      ii. Posting (largest to smallest)

      iii. Advocacy (reverse alphabetically, or Z to A)

   B. Once finished sorting, alter targets' Motivation scores (as desired) based on job posting quality, advocacy contacts, or additional research of unknown employers. Then re-sort. Repeat until satisfied with Top 5. (Your final list should resemble the sample on page 80.)

Part 2: Contact Boosters, Obligates, and Curmudgeons

6. Naturalize (20 minutes)

   A. Identify two starter contacts using the following order of recommended priority for each Top 5 employer:

      i. Functionally relevant

      ii. Fellow alumni (or affinity group member)

     iii. One to two levels above where you'd start

     iv. Internally promoted

     v. Uniquely named

B. Identify method for contacting them using the following order of recommended priority:

     i. LinkedIn Groups

     ii. Direct email:

        a. Alumni (or affinity) database

        b. Email finders (e.g., Hunter.io)

        c. "Fan mail"

     iii. LinkedIn invitations to connect

     iv. Facebook/Twitter/other social media

     v. LinkedIn second-degree connections

7. Email (20 minutes)

A. Draft 6-Point Email to favorite starter contact at each Top 5 employer:

     i. Write fewer than seventy-five words.

     ii. Ask for insight and advice, not job leads.

     iii. State your connection first.

     iv. Make your request in the form of a question (ending in "?").

     v. Define your interest both narrowly and broadly.

     vi. Keep over half the word count about the *contact*, not about you.

8. Track (10 minutes)

   A. Follow the 3B7 Routine for Top 5 target employers:

      i. Set two reminders in your email program's calendar *every time* a 6-Point Email is sent to a new contact for the first time:

         a. 3B reminder: Try someone else

         b. 7B reminder: Follow up

   B. Initiate contact with a new target employer beyond your Top 5 anytime:

      i. A true Booster has been identified at one of your Top 5 (rendering further new effort at that employer unnecessary).

      ii. An employer is ruled out.

      iii. Time permits (once you've completed outreach to a third contact at each of your initial Top 5 using 3B7 correctly).

Part 3: Convince: Informational Meetings

9. Research (~15 minutes per interview)

   A. Conduct external research:

      i. See investor relations pages on employer websites.

      ii. Review positive headlines on front page of target's website.

      iii. Google both employer (for any negative headlines) and interviewer.

B. Prepare for the Big Four:

    i. "Tell me about yourself."

    ii. "Why do you want to work for our organization?"

    iii. "Why do you want to work in this role?"

    iv. "Why do you want to work in our sector/industry?"

10. Discuss (~30 minutes per interview)

A. Movement #1: Small talk. Small talk should occur naturally, but can be induced systematically if it does not:

    i. "How is your day going so far?"

    ii. "What's been your path to joining <organization>?"

    iii. "What are you working on right now?"

B. Movement #2: Questions and answers (TIARA):

    i. Trends

    ii. Insights

    iii. Advice

    iv. Resources

    v. Assignments

Expert ⬇ Mentor ⬇

C. Movement #3: Next steps:

    i. If a referral is offered, commit (and schedule) yourself to follow up in two weeks.

    ii. If a referral is not offered, transition to Two-Part Informational Closing

11. Follow-up (Ongoing)

A. Follow Harvest Cycle to update those with whom you've conducted informationals on a monthly basis.

ACKNOWLEDGMENTS

The one common perspective shared by the best job seekers I encounter is that the job search is about others, not themselves. You need the help of others to get opportunities as well as the support of others to keep you sane en route. I myself would like to thank some people who gave me this opportunity and kept me sane en route:

- My family—I truly couldn't have done this without your support.

- My agent, Richard Morris—thank you for your years of steady insight and confidence in this book's potential.

- My editors, Sara Golski, Kimmy Tejasindhu, and Julie Bennett at Ten Speed Press—how you made this readable, I have no idea!

- Amanda Ray—you were everything from coach to editor to business manager to personal advocate for me while bringing this book to life, and for that I am eternally grateful.

- Dan Heath—you were the first person who never doubted this project's potential, and your mentorship throughout has been invaluable.

- Peter DiCola, Tim Nangle, Jean Ro, Javier Izquierdo, Brett Lasher, Becca Gonzales, and Melissa Gudell—for everything.

- My amazing Career Management Center colleagues at Fuqua, past and present—I've relied upon and learned from you every day for over a decade, and without your mentorship, knowledge, and support, this book simply would not exist. From the bottom of my heart, thank you.

- Three Fuqua colleagues in particular: Jennifer Fink, David Solloway, and Shawn Pulscher—your constant stream of questions, ideas, and general brilliance are really what made a revised edition both possible and necessary. Thank you for consistently pushing the envelope, seeing what *could* be, and working toward a better tomorrow for our profession. You have *no idea* how much I appreciate it.

- Professor Dan Ariely—without your insight on social versus market norms, this process likely never would have gone beyond LAMP.

- Tom Cal—thank you for helping me customize this process for transitioning military veterans.

- Jessica Thomas—thank you for sharing you own book-publishing experiences with me when I was just getting started.

- Mike Stracco—I've had many great teachers over the years, but I never would have developed my writing voice without your AP English class. Thank you.

- Beth Corcoran, Ankur Seth, Roger Austin, and Jeremy Schifeling—you each customized this process in an important way in its early days, so thank you for your collaboration.

- Veronica Ho, Ivan Kerbel, and Vic Menon—thank you for your advocacy and belief in my material when I was getting under way so, so many years ago.

- All of my Facebook brainstormers—you never let me down when I was in need of an analogy or idea.

- The city of Durham, North Carolina.

NOTES

Introduction

1. https://www.newyorkfed.org/medialibrary/media/research/staff_reports/sr568.pdf.

2. Gail Matthews and Pauline Rose Clance, "Treatment of the Impostor Phenomenon in Psychotherapy Clients," *Psychotherapy in Private Practice* 3, no. 1 (1985): 71–81, DOI: 10.1300/J294v03n01_09.

3. https://web.archive.org/web/20021218011841/https://www.microsoft.com/mscorp/execmail/2002/10-02customers.asp.

Chapter 1

1. https://www.census.gov/quickfacts/fact/table/losalamoscdpnewmexico/PST045218; https://www.lanl.gov/about/facts-figures/index.php.

Chapter 3

1. Dan Ariely's book *Predictably Irrational* (New York: Harper Perennial, 2010) explores the concept of arbitrary coherence very effectively.

Chapter 5

2. Mark S. Granovetter, "The Strength of Weak Ties," *American Journal of Sociology* 78, no. 6 (May 1973): 1360–80.

Chapter 9

1. Benjamin Franklin, *The Autobiography of Benjamin Franklin* (New York: Henry Holt Company, 1916).

2. J. Jecker and D. Landy, "Liking a Person as Function of Doing Him a Favor," *Human Relations* 22 (1969): 371–78, http://changingminds.org/explanations/theories/ben_franklin_effect.htm.

3. K. Huang, M. Yeomans, A.W. Brooks, J. Minson, and F. Gino, "It Doesn't Hurt to Ask: Question-Asking Increases Liking," *Journal of Personality and Social Psychology* 113, no. 3 (September 2017): 430–52.

4. Robert B. Cialdini, *Influence: The Psychology of Persuasion* (New York: HarperCollins, 1984).

Conclusion

1. Robert S. Welch, "The Fosbury Flop Is Still a Big Hit," *Sports Illustrated*, September 12, 1988, 22–25.

2. Chip and Dan Heath, *Switch* (New York: Random House, 2010).

ABOUT THE AUTHOR

STEVE DALTON is the founder and CEO of corporate training firm Contact2Colleague, and a senior career consultant and program director at Duke University's Fuqua School of Business. He holds an MBA from the same institution. Prior to entering the career services industry, Steve was a twice-promoted strategy consultant with A. T. Kearney and an associate marketing manager at General Mills. He lives in Durham, North Carolina. Visit www.2hourjobsearch.com and www.contact2colleague.com for inquiries, follow Steve on Twitter at @Dalton_Steve, and join the book's LinkedIn Group at "The 2-Hour Job Search—Q&A Forum."

INDEX